Dear Paul, Am I On The Right Track?

Dear Paul, Am I On The Right Track?

RON SMITH &
ROB PENNER

YWAM Publishing
A Ministry of Youth With A Mission
P.O. Box 55787, Seattle, WA 98155
(206) 771-1153

Dear Paul, Am I On the Right Track?
Copyright © 1993 by Ron Smith & Rob Penner

Published by YWAM Publishing, a division of Youth With A Mission; P. O. Box 55787, Seattle, WA 98155

ISBN 0-927545-58-6

Dedication

To Judy and Joy,
our best friends,
best critics,
and greatest fans.

With deep gratitude....

Together, we would like to thank all of the School of Biblical Studies staff and students who have helped us examine ourselves and the Church in light of the Bible's view on spirituality.

We also thank "Pulitzer Prize nominee" Scott Tompkins for editing this book.

Ron would like to say thank you to Sam Wilson, David Ross, John Kuhne, David Zbikowski, Rich Wells, and Alec Lindley. You have kept my feet on the ground, and have made me laugh.

Table of Contents

Introduction

Maybe you have never laid your hands on the sick to see them recover. Or perhaps you suffer from a sickness and have not yet been healed. You might be a crummy evangelist, inconsistent in your prayer life, and never have cast out a demon. When you compare such a spiritual midget to the giants of the faith, you probably feel somewhat inferior.

All too often, spirituality is rated according to experience. Maybe you have met someone who thought you weren't really spiritual unless you prophesy regularly, speak in tongues, abstain from television, cast out demons, or live in health and financial prosperity. Others go to the opposite extreme and assign spiritual status to things they consider virtues, like poverty and pain—those who are truly spiritual truly suffer.

The apostle Paul wrote many letters to correct such excesses of the first-century Church. But as the sinful heart of man causes history to endlessly repeat itself, these same problems remain in our twentieth-century Church. Paul's letters remain with us to provide balance and direction in the endless maze of diverse teachings.

Imagine if Paul lived in the United States today. How would he respond to the extremes of doctrine gushing forth from our pulpits? His rebukes, warnings, encouragements, and exhortations would probably be similar to the ones he gave in the first century.

One New Testament letter that seems to be particularly relevant to the twentieth-century Church is the one written to the Colossian church. In first century Colossae, the Church was grappling with its spiritual identity. Believers there thought that their spirituality would be enhanced by the most thrilling spiritual experiences. The result was a conglomeration of beliefs, each tenet stemming from one person's experience. Today's diversity in beliefs, many of which are also based in experience, is equally astounding. How is a sincere Christian supposed to find his way?

Christians believe that seekers of truth need only turn to God's Word to find answers. A young Christian named Madeline is such a seeker. She has just moved, with her husband and two boys, from Boston to Los Angeles. She is struggling to find spiritual truth among the myriad of strange beliefs she finds there. For help she turns to Paul Lombardy, the elderly pastor who first guided her to Christ two months earlier in Boston.

Their letters to each other form the basis of this book. Though the characters are fictional, most of Madeline's experiences, as well as those of Paul, are based on true situations. If you have ever wondered if you're spiritual enough, you're likely to find the answer in the following pages. We hope this book guides you to a true revelation of Christ, and a new sense of who you are in Him.

1

Your Friendly Neighborhood Colossians

Dear Pastor Paul,

*W*ell, I'm glad that move is over! Most of the boxes are unpacked, and our new apartment is finally in some semblance of order. I wish I could say the same for myself.

Not that I'm the basket case you met three months ago. I really miss the support of everyone there in Boston, especially yours. Los Angeles will take some getting used to (cough, wheeze), and I'd give almost anything to be back in Boston with my friends. Of all my 31 years on the planet, this past one has been the toughest. You and the church were like a few months of calm sunshine in the middle of a long, dark storm.

The storm seems like it's raging pretty strong again. Four mornings out of five, I wake up feeling depressed about my parents' deaths. Feelings of grief get a little old after ten months. And just when I think that I've forgiven that drunk driver, I imagine myself meeting him on the street. In my darkest moments, he gets full recompense for what he did.

Lee is gone quite a bit on his new sales route. He's a great support when he's home, but he's more often away. I'm trying to be both mom and dad to the kids. Andrew's asthma isn't helped by the smog of Los Angeles, and we've already paid the clinic a few visits. Two-year-old Joey is one carefree bright spot in my turmoil.

I am trying to read through the New Testament like you suggested. I'm not ready to enter a theological debate with a non-Christian yet, but I do feel like I'm beginning to understand Jesus more. I don't know if I'll ever be like Him, but I certainly do need Him. If it weren't for my faith in Christ, I honestly think I would be scaling a ledge somewhere in downtown Los Angeles right now.

Where would I be if I hadn't met you? I thank God often that our washing machines broke down at the same time. Imagine—a Boston laundromat served as the crossroads for my life! I ask an unassuming old gentleman (I still can't believe you're 78!) for a quarter, and end up sharing the burdens of my heart. Who would have thought that getting some small change would end up in such a big change for me?

You not only taught me about Jesus, you became the father I had just lost. I remember my dad answering all the silly questions I could put to him as a child. I guess as a new Christian, my childlike questions were equally as silly. Thanks for taking all the time with me.

I guess you're probably wondering where all this sentimental gush is coming from. I'm not really sure myself, but I do miss you and all my friends there at the church. Getting the news of Lee's job transfer was a tough blow.

When you warned that I was moving to a spiritual Disneyland, I really had no idea what to expect. So far I have been on one very strange ride, and have met someone who seems to be from Space Mountain. It all began when I attended a church that was listed in the newspaper. This is the last time I will use the "close my eyes and point" method when selecting a church!

The church you started in Boston is the only one I have ever been to, and I assumed that most Christian churches would be similar. Boy, was I wrong! I felt totally uncomfortable at Freedom Tabernacle, and it wasn't because of the hard pews. I kept feeling like people were expecting me to do something. It reminded me of a TV variety show. I was the only one in my pew who failed to go up front either for ministry or to give a testimony or prophecy.

I tried to slip out quickly after the final chorus, but three ladies stopped me to chat before I could get away. Our conversation didn't get too far past the weather in Los Angeles, rush hour traffic, and the day's smog count, but they kept staring at my face as if I had my makeup smeared or something.

Imagine my surprise when one of them phoned me on Tuesday. Her name was Geraldine Cabot. I had forgotten her name, but not her booming, drill sergeant's voice that seemed to demand obedience.

This time Geraldine skipped the small talk and got right to the purpose of her call. She said that she and her friends had felt led to invite me to a deliverance session. I had never heard that term in your church, and I guessed that a deliverance session was a church-sponsored Lamaze class. It occurred to me that they must have thought I was pregnant.

But she wasn't talking about baby delivery at all. Through our brief chat on Sunday morning, the three ladies had concluded that I am demon possessed! They were offering to cast it out of me.

At first, I was too shocked to know whether I should thank them or be offended. My first thought was that of a little girl's head spinning around on her shoulders. That's what happened to the demon-possessed girl in *The Exorcist,* a movie I saw many years ago. This was the sum total of my knowledge about demons.

I tried to put Geraldine off and get some time to collect my thoughts, but she was absolutely insistent that I attend this week's session. She told me to stop hiding from God, and that the longer I wait, the greater Satan's stronghold would be in my life.

To that I had no answer whatsoever. She knew I was a new Christian, and told me very pointedly that she had been a Christian since before I was born. How should I have responded, Pastor Paul? Could I really be demon possessed?

I was able to get off the phone when Joey woke from his nap and began crying. But I haven't been able to get Geraldine's words out of my mind. The part that really bothers me is about Satan gaining a greater stronghold in my life. I thought that I was giving more and more of myself to God. If what Geraldine said is true, it kind of turns the whole thing into a game between God and Satan, and makes me feel like a very useless player.

I think I'm most upset that one measly phone call could shake me up so bad. I know better than anyone that my life isn't perfect...but demon possessed? I had gotten used to the thought that God is in control of my life, making all the misshapen pieces of the puzzle somehow fit together. If I lose that comfort, I honestly don't have much at all.

I know, I'm going on and on. But I need your assurance that my newfound hope and security aren't just an illusion. Geraldine made me feel like I'm not really a Christian at all. She didn't come right out and say that, but I definitely felt like she was trying to convert me.

Pastor Paul, do I still need to be converted to something? I want to get settled in a church here in L.A., but it won't be Freedom Tabernacle. On the bright side, I have learned one thing in this experience: never fill out the guest card on your first Sunday in a new church.

Your friend, Madeline

Dear Onesimus,

*B*efore you think I am a forgetful old man who can't remember your name, let me explain "Onesimus" to you. Your situation reminds me of his. You see, when the apostle Paul was an old man and imprisoned in Rome, he met a young man named Onesimus and led him to faith in Christ. This young man became very dear to Paul, just as you have become to me. (You're not the only one who can throw out "sentimental gush.")

Paul taught and nurtured Onesimus in Rome. But the young man had a great problem, much worse than moving to L.A. Onesimus was a runaway slave (and probably a thief), which meant, for him, the possibility of the death sentence. When he left his friend Paul and went back to his old master in Colossae, he was probably very scared and lonely. Paul sent a letter of recommendation back with him to his old master, Philemon, who was also one of Paul's converts. At the same time, he sent another letter to the church that met in Philemon's house. This second one is the New Testament letter called "Colossians."

If Los Angeles is a spiritual Disneyland, then Colossae would have been its first-century counterpart. Your conversation with Geraldine left you mystified, like you had just entered an unknown realm. She sounds like someone who depends heavily on transcendent experiences. But as Onesimus can surely tell you when you see him in heaven, Geraldine Cabot is not the first mystic to grace our planet.

During the days of Onesimus, mystery religions began to flourish. These were exclusive clubs that generally accepted new members only after they fulfilled elaborate initiation rites. One group—called the cult of Mithras—placed newcomers under a grate in a hole in the ground. A bull was pulled on top of the grate, slain, and sliced open. The initiate received a warm shower with bull's blood.

You're probably wondering why I'm comparing Geraldine Cabot to this cult of Mithras. Well, both expect newcomers to do something before they can be qualified for fellowship. After undergoing an initiation ceremony, members of the mystery cults were expected to have many visions and supernatural experiences. This was the way they moved up the spiritual ladder, becoming marked as the spiritual giants of the group.

In the first century, this kind of thinking quickly

moved into the Colossian church. Onesimus left his spiritual father in Rome and returned to a group of Christians who were frantically searching for more revelations. The "most successful" were the ones who could have the most revelations.

When Paul wrote to the Colossian church, he discussed the concept of mystery. He told those who spent their days seeking a new vision that the true mystery is one that everyone can experience. In fact, the real mystery is not that mysterious at all. It is simply the fact that Christ lives inside those of us who believe in Him.

From the way you have described her, Geraldine Cabot sounds like a classic Colossian. She concluded that you were demon possessed from just one brief chat about smog. She is someone that we would call a mystic.

Now don't get me wrong, Madeline. There is a place for mysticism in the church. After all, God is spirit, and He communicates with us spiritually. The problem comes when we give mysticism too great a place in our thinking. I've heard many stories about people who think they've heard God say He will heal their incurable sickness, only to succumb to it later. Families have been heartbroken and even unprepared to continue without the one they were certain would be healed. Placing all of one's hopes in a spiritual voice can be dangerous.

The same can be said of demon-chasers like Geraldine. I wouldn't worry over her mystical speculations about your spirituality. In times past, I've had people in my church who see demons everywhere. To them, every problem from car trouble to cigarette addiction needs deliverance. Maybe Geraldine thought you needed to have the spirit of disliking smog cast out of you.

Like you said, the greater problem is that a lady with a strong voice has caused you to question your spirituality. As you meet more Christians, you are going to discover that there are more brands of Christianity than there are breakfast cereals. And each one is convinced that their brand is the most spiritually nutritious. First and foremost, remember that you are justified by faith in Christ, not by a secondary spiritual experience. People that promote mystical experiences above Jesus have trivialized the work of Christ.

It must have been a struggle for Onesimus to know what true spirituality was. Paul used letters to instruct his spiritual children. In the same way, I'd like to be your Paul in Boston, and you can be my Onesimus in L.A. During my years in ministry, I've seen a lot of people chasing after extremes in the name of Jesus. Maybe I can help explain some of the strange rides you find yourself on in your spiritual Disneyland.

Believe me, Madeline, this is not a game, and you are certainly not a useless player. The name *Onesimus* means "useful." Paul said that the former slave attained the meaning of his name through the redemption of Christ. The same thing could be said of you, regardless of what mystics like Geraldine Cabot think.

So, my Onesimus out there in "La-La Land," be strong in Christ. I pray that He will lead you to a home church that is not too much of a "wild" ride.

Your brother in Christ, Paul

Dear Pastor Paul,

*T*hanks for the letter and even for retaliating with some of your own sentimental gush. I'm glad that I can put Geraldine Cabot and the people at Freedom Tabernacle out of my mind without feeling that I'm missing something. My New Testament reading this week was in Mark 5, the story about an uncontrollable demoniac who lived in caves and liked to cut himself on sharp rocks. I hope the three ladies weren't thinking I am like him!

This week I took little Joey out to the park by our apartment. A lady named Sunset, who lives in the same complex, was there with her son, too. The kids hit it off nicely and played together for a good two hours.

Sunset is like the kind of person I expected every young Californian woman to be like. The front few strands of her long blond hair are braided on either side of her face. Her voice has that Valley Girl quality that I had only seen on television. Most of all, she's philosophical in a bubbly, spacey kind of way.

I'm glad you explained about mystics to me in your last letter. It really prepared me to meet and understand Sunset. I'm not totally sure she's a Christian, but I felt better about being with her than I would have with Geraldine Cabot. Sunset is less intimidating, more accepting. Still, she does have some interesting ideas that I hadn't heard before.

Sunset believes that Christ lives inside her consciousness. Other than the wording, that's pretty much the same thing that we believe. She went on to say that Jesus has grown into her mind through meditation. According to her, Jesus is a product of her focused imagination, and has taken on a personality that is unique to her. She perceives Him through yoga and other spiritual exercises. Maybe some of these aren't too different from the quiet times you encouraged me to have.

She does think that Jesus is God, but then again she

thinks that she is, too. In fact, Sunset thinks that everyone is a god, including me. That's by far the highest compliment I've had in a while. She says that her mission in life is to find the spark of divinity inside her, and fan it into a flame. I got the impression that Jesus is her example of how to do that.

I remember when yoga became popular in the '70s. I tried to do it once, but gave up because my legs hurt so bad from being in that position. I couldn't meditate on anything besides the pain. But what about Sunset's beliefs? Is she living in the Twilight Zone, too? I could really use a friend right now. Having an extended conversation with an adult was like eating a meal after a month with no food.

Boy, it's been a month since I said goodbye to you and the others in Boston. Sometimes it seems like a day, sometimes like a year. The world of Los Angeles is different in so many ways. I'm not quite sure how I fit in, but I get the impression it would be impossible to be out of place. So far, it seems there are all kinds here.

Your L.A. Onesimus

Dear L.A. Onesimus,

So you've gone from being a demoniac one week to being a deity the next. Quite a promotion, I would say. Your new friend sounds like a nice lady. But even though Sunset may have a sweet disposition, she's much further from the truth than Geraldine Cabot.

Sunset's understanding of Jesus is of the New Age variety. To the New Ager, Jesus was an example of an ordinary man who understood His deity.

Actually, Madeline, this is similar to the heresy that entered the Colossian church. Onesimus returned to Colossae just in time to hear some very bizarre teaching. Like Sunset, the false teachers in Colossae believed that a spark of divinity lay dormant inside each person. With the help of visions and angels, this spark could turn into a divine fire.

Now I hate to be the one who steals the highest compliment you've gotten, but please don't think of yourself as deity. You certainly are a nice person, and I have come to think of you as a daughter...but Jesus is the only God who has walked the earth. When Paul wrote to the Colossians, he said that "[Jesus] is the head of the body, the church; he is the beginning and the firstborn from among the dead, so that in everything he might have the supremacy."

At best, the false teachers thought of Jesus as an example. Mostly they considered Him a phantom or an angel—the doorway to divine experiences. Paul wrote to them chiefly to establish the place Jesus needed to have in their thinking. He cannot be reduced to an angelic Captain Kirk taking His spaceship called the Church on a spiritual Star Trek.

Jesus has always been a popular person, even among unbelievers. Many people have wanted to plug Him into their way of thinking, hoping to justify their ideas. I recently read something by a well-educated theologian who liked studying UFO's. He somehow "discovered" various times in the New Testament in which Jesus encountered extraterrestrial creatures. In fact, do you remember reading about the cloud that carried Jesus into heaven in front of the disciples' eyes? You guessed it—a UFO of the cumulus kind.

Your new friend, Sunset, is doing the same thing. She has plugged Jesus into her New Age way of thinking. To her, Jesus is probably not that different from herself, perhaps just a little more progressive. But the Jesus that you have come to know and believe in is your Master and Owner.

I'm sorry if this puts Sunset in a bad light. But the friendship of Jesus is worth more than a thousand friends here on earth. I can empathize with the loneliness you are feeling in your city. When my wife, Gracie, passed away three years ago, I felt like I lost part of my body. Even though I was surrounded by a few million people in Boston, I felt like I was all alone.

That time of unbearable loneliness was one of the most important times in my life. I experienced the friendship of Jesus more than I ever had before. I know you want some good friends at this time in your life, Madeline. I'll be praying that in His time, God will give you some. But take advantage of your loneliness by drawing near to your Lord Jesus. He's the one who will personally walk through every experience you have.

Your friend, Paul

Dear Pastor Paul,

I got your letter on Tuesday morning, then happened to run into Sunset that afternoon. Hoping to explain Jesus more clearly to her, I invited her to come up for coffee after our boys finished their naps.

I mostly just shared my testimony. She nodded cheerfully as I talked, and said that my experiences were "most excellent." I guess I was a little surprised. I mean, I thought if we disagreed about something, she might at least try to slip in her view. She's not exactly the shy type. But you know what? She actually called herself a Christian, and I proceeded to pat myself on the back.

Then Sunset went on to talk about her own life some more. She said that since she developed her Christ consciousness, she just doesn't seem to have any more hassles. She's living with a guy right now who has helped her learn how to develop the spiritual side of her life. Her two-year-old son was fathered by another man about four boyfriends ago.

This news really repulsed me, especially since our children were playing together. So I asked her if she wasn't ever bothered about being so promiscuous. I told her that raising a two-year-old in a home like hers wasn't really fair to the child. Furthermore, I added, her lifestyle was definitely not fitting for a Christian. I guess I'm not the shy type, either.

Sunset said that her lifestyle wasn't anyone else's business. In fact, she thought I needed to be more open-minded and accepting of others. "That's what Jesus is like," she added.

Then I made what was probably a big mistake—I brought up the subject of hell. I didn't actually know very much about hell, so it may not have been the wisest thing to talk about. I remembered you explaining it to me when I committed my life to Christ.

Sunset thinks that hell is the worst thing anyone has ever thought up. We Christians make it to heaven, while all the sinners, Buddhists, Hindus, and Muslims go in the other direction. She said all that does is make some people feel superior and others feel like worms. Heaven, she said, is her reality, and it's the place she's in right now. It's a state of mind. It's a big place, big enough for every religion and lifestyle in the world.

My talk was obviously taking her out of her mental paradise, because she grabbed her son and walked out in huff. Now I feel like the narrow-minded person she said I was. After all, who am I to say what the eternal destiny of people should be? And what right do I have to judge someone's lifestyle?

What you said in your last letter about Sunset's perception of Jesus was right on. It seems like you know her better than I do. But all the same, doesn't she have a point? Aren't we being narrow-minded? Is it fair to say that our ideas about Jesus are the only way to life?

I guess Sunset won't be over again. So much for my attempt at being Miss Evangelist.

Your L.A. Onesimus

Dear L.A. Onesimus,

I applaud your narrow-mindedness. Christians are at once the most accepting and the most narrow people in the world. Jesus freely gave His time to the darkest of sinners. But He also said that He is the way, the truth, and the life, and that no one could come to the Father except by Him. We are as narrow as the One we follow.

Remember how I compared your situation to Onesimus and the Colossian church? Sunset's idea of embracing different belief systems was also part of the Colossian problem. That church had a variety of members from different backgrounds, creating a hodgepodge of spiritual beliefs.

Imagine what it was like for Onesimus to walk in on this crowd. First, he noticed the legalists. Those were Jews in skull caps and long beards, looking quite disturbed about the dirty toenails walking through the door. In another section, he saw the rationalists. Those philosophical Greeks argued about spiritual reality. Many believed Plato's teaching that "the body is the prison of the soul," so they tortured their bodies to get closer to God. Then there were the extreme mystics who broke out of their dreamland only long enough to challenge everyone else in the church with their vision.

Poor Onesimus! He must have felt like he had just set foot on Mars. He probably felt quite a bit like you're feeling right now.

It would be tempting to pat Sunset on the back, encourage her beliefs, and remain friendly. We should make the same effort to be open that she is, right?

Paul mostly wrote to the Colossians about Jesus, and encouraged everyone in the church to be built up in Him. He told them pointedly that only Jesus is God, and that they are made blameless through His work. Paul didn't write a treatise on how people with different ideas can walk in brotherhood. He wrote about how they should relate to Jesus. If they do that correctly, they can walk in unity. As a body needs a head to function, so the Church must lift up Jesus to walk in unity.

Let me tell you that I am very proud of the way you spoke with Sunset. Maybe the poor girl has never had anyone tell her that she's living a sinful life. You presented her with the reality of Jesus, even though she thinks there is no such thing as objective truth. Good job...Miss Evangelist.

Keep reading through the New Testament, and

you'll become more secure in what you believe. You'll find that the truth has boundaries and makes demands of us. In fighting these boundaries and demands, Sunset is opposing the truth.

Nearly all mistakes in spiritual perception stem from one point of ignorance: misunderstanding who Jesus was and what He accomplished. As you are searching for a church, find out if they believe in the deity of Christ, His virgin birth, His atoning death for mankind, and His resurrection. It is also critical that they believe the Bible is God's Word to man.

You may have driven away your one almost-friend in Los Angeles. But look at it this way—at least you planted one seed of truth in a field of weedy deception. Who knows? Maybe that seed will grow and turn into something profitable for Sunset and the Kingdom of God.

Keep being narrow. It's the only way to go.

Your friend, Paul

Dear Pastor Paul,

*T*o be honest, I didn't mind so much that Sunset left my apartment upset. For one thing, the more she talked, the more flaky I could see she was. How could a together person go through so many men? I don't think I could handle a friend like that yet.

Geraldine Cabot phoned back this week. She turned out to be just the mystic you had described. When I asked her why she thought I was demon possessed, she said that she just had a sense that something wasn't right about me. I told her that I had the same sense about her. I know it wasn't the kindest thing to say, but it sure felt good at the time. She didn't take that very well at all, which leads me to believe that she won't phone again.

Later, I thought about the situation some more. How can I be absolutely sure that Geraldine is wrong? I would think that she has spent a lot of years learning to hear God's voice. If she and I were competing in a spirituality contest, even I would place my money on her.

I would like to begin developing my spirituality more. I know that Sunset's spiritual life is not the Christian kind, but what about Geraldine's? Personally, I would hate the thought of approaching a stranger and telling her that she is demon possessed. I couldn't even tell her that her stockings were ripped! But maybe passing on spiritual insights about others is part of learning to trust God.

Is that what it means to be a spiritual person? So far in my Christian life, I have just been receiving the comfort of Christ, and this has been very important to me. But I am getting the impression that there should be something more.

I haven't really been looking very hard for a home church. It's not that I'm lazy or anything. I guess I'm embarrassed by my babyhood, like I know so much less than everyone else. With you folks in Boston, I was expected to be ignorant and inexperienced. Even though I still am both of those things, I somehow feel that I should be moving on to more spiritual experiences.

As far as other things go, my grief over my parents is slowly beginning to subside. You were right about Jesus being a close friend in times of loneliness. I really do feel His presence. It's been about two months since we arrived in Los Angeles, and Lee is still gone most of the time. He insists that this will change in a few weeks, once he gets to know all his customers.

Well, my debut in Los Angeles has been far from illustrious—two months, two people who want to spend time with me, and now two people who don't like me. I imagine that your advice to me right now would be to cheer up. Things could only get better.

Your L.A. Onesimus

Dear L.A. Onesimus,

*B*y your questions I can see that your two "friends" have gotten to you. In fact, your introspective probing is beginning to make you sound like a Colossian. Their biggest problem (which resulted from dethroning Christ) was to seek ways of enhancing their spirituality. The supernatural experiences of a minority and a few fringe beliefs became the standard for judging normal spirituality.

The Colossians bred a proud, competitive spirit. You mentioned being in a spirituality contest with Geraldine. That is Colossian thinking in its truest and most dangerous form. The super-spiritual in the church disqualified the weaker members, making them feel they lacked something in their Christian experience. Paul said in Colossians 2:18,19, "Do not let anyone who delights in false humility and the worship of angels disqualify you for the prize. Such a person goes into great detail about what he has seen, and his unspiritual mind puffs him up with idle notions."

So one group in the church thought they had a corner on God and spiritual experiences. They are the ones who lifted their noses proudly and said, "I am so very, very spiritual." The other group groveled at the other extreme. They observed the great experiences of the super-spiritual and lamented, "I'm just not spiritual enough."

Similarly today, Christians are always expecting unrealistic things from other Christians. You'll read books, hear sermons, and talk to friends who will tell you what you must do to be really spiritual. Depending on who you listen to or what you read, you'll find that you need to fast one day a week, speak in tongues, pray for an hour each day (preferably on your knees), cast out demons, witness to people who intimidate you, receive inner healing, receive physical healing, have visions, confess each sin publicly, and submit to the Lord's anointed (unless he fails to do any of the above). With a load like this, I would have to kiss my retirement plan goodbye.

Of course you know that I think all of these things are good within reason. But the point is that Jesus seldom causes us to question our spirituality. Usually other Christians are the culprits.

Sometimes we place unrealistic expectations on ourselves. I remember that when I was in seminary, I tried to spend lengthy times in prayer. I thought that kneeling was the most spiritual prayer position, so I knelt on a pillow beside my bed each day. Then I heard that James, the Lord's brother and leader of the first-century church in Jerusalem, was nicknamed "Camel Knees" because of the calluses from all the hours he spent in prayer. He certainly didn't use a pillow. So I quit using the cushion and tried to be as spiritual as James. My knees were somewhat less tough than a camel's, so the experiment didn't last long. I won't say that this small failure devastated me, but it did reinforce the concept that I was just not spiritual enough.

Paul's advice to the Colossians is appropriate for you to consider: "...You have been given fullness in Christ, who is the head over every power and authority." In other words, Madeline, right now you are as spiritual as you will ever be. You don't need to be locked inside a visionary trance or hear God tell you that your neighbor is demon possessed before you can consider yourself spiritual. You have been made spiritual through the work of Christ already done in your life. As you learn that Jesus is your Head, the source of your life, then you will grow into an understanding of your spirituality.

It sounds like your relationship with Jesus is good and growing. That is sufficient for true spirituality. My advice is simply to continue getting to know Jesus better. Don't waste your time chasing after spiritual experiences. Instead, seek Jesus through prayer and Bible study. He will give you the experiences of His choosing.

I don't think your debut in Los Angeles has been that bad. Just think about some of the difficult things you were up against. After all, Geraldine Cabot would not be my choice for a welcoming committee. I think you stood up amazingly well through it all. And the difficulties and questions are causing you to grow into a strong, spiritual woman of God.

Your friend, Paul

2

They Know More Than You

Dear Paul,

*T*he days are passing slowly here as I find myself less and less inclined to go outside and meet people. Apart from the occasional visit to Andrew's school, I mostly just hibernate at home. After Geraldine and Sunset, I have my doubts that I can relate to anyone here in Los Angeles.

I spend most of my free time reading the Bible and watching television. Sometimes I do both at the same time by following Bible studies taught by TV preachers. I guess that's my church right now. Anyway, my questions for you this time are not about the Bible or even TV preachers. I want to ask you about something else I saw on television.

The other night, Lee and I watched a movie based

on the life of a famous actress. She has become one of the New Age movement's chief spokespersons. As I watched the show, it became clear to me where Sunset got the idea that she is a god.

Anyway, this actress did not seem as flaky as Sunset. She spoke so confidently and persuasively that I found it difficult to imagine that she may be deceived. I thought of her in the same light as yourself—a mature leader who knows what she believes. I guess if I carried that comparison a little further, I could compare Sunset to myself, a shaky novice who is not a great representation of her faith.

Lee was impressed with how this lady in the movie had gained her knowledge. She grew in her spirituality as she passed through spiritual experiences, being taught by gurus and listening to her spirit guide. I think Lee appreciates the fact that she's not as exclusive as Christians tend to be. She was tolerant in the same way that I found Sunset to be. I explained to him your thoughts on that.

My husband has seen how my faith in Jesus has given me strength during some difficult times. He also sees how this actress' faith has strengthened her. He thought that her experiences were interesting, and that the teaching she now possesses is valid. I find the thought of her spiritual knowledge intimidating. I have this nightmare about her having dinner at our house and converting me with no arguments.

So, what about her knowledge? How can I tell if it's valid or not? And what should I tell Lee, who seems to lean more to this lady's beliefs than to mine?

It is nice to have my husband home. He doesn't have a trip for a few weeks. Maybe I'll get out a bit now. If I had the money, I would pop over to Boston for a visit, but for now, all we can afford is a stamp.

Your L.A. Onesimus

Dear L.A. Onesimus,

I'm glad you're able to work a stamp into your budget. Our letters are becoming like a correspondence course in spirituality. Stick with what you believe, and in the end, you won't be intimidated by even the biggest deceived movie star.

Do you remember how shaky you felt on the first day of a new job? I recall my first week as a carpenter's apprentice years before I entered the ministry. My fingers were so bruised and bloodied that day. It's no wonder—I hit them more often than I hit the nail! But my boss was patient with me as I hurt myself, bent nails, and made crooked cuts. Like a newcomer to any field, I grew in my carpentry skills as I gained knowledge and experience.

In the same way, Madeline, the Bible teaches Christians to "grow in the grace and knowledge of our Lord and Savior Jesus Christ." For us, spiritual growth must have the knowledge of Christ as its goal. The actress you saw on television has a different goal: building up her own spirituality. She is doing this by gaining "knowledge" through spiritual experiences.

Let me give you a lesson this week on "knowledge." Our English word *know* comes from the Greek word *gnosis*. In the first few centuries after Jesus walked the earth, cult groups began springing up teaching something called *gnosticism*. The thinking of these gnostics affected the Colossian church. They taught that one must have a special knowledge in order to be delivered from sin. Much like the actress you saw, these gnostics gained this special knowledge through elaborate rituals and visionary experiences.

This would have been very difficult for the new believer Onesimus to face. He must have felt every bit as intimidated as you would feel with the famous actress at your house. These gnostics in Colossae were bursting with knowledge (or so they called it) from their experiences. For a new believer like Onesimus, talking to them would have been similar to you or me discussing brain surgery with a neurosurgeon.

Paul told the Colossians to beware of the traps of these "enlightened" super saints. Read his instruction from Colossians 2:8:

See to it that no one takes you captive through hollow and deceptive philosophy, which depends on human tradition and the basic principles of this world rather than on Christ.

According to the New Testament, anyone who confesses Christ as Lord is already in possession of this special knowledge. Paul told the Colossians that in Jesus "are hidden all the treasures of wisdom and knowledge."

The apostle Peter also wrote to churches infiltrated by gnostics. To these churches he said, "His divine power has given us everything we need for life and godliness through our knowledge of him..." (II Peter 1:3). Madeline, your knowledge of Christ has given you everything you need for life.

Realize that you are still a new Christian. Only accept those messages that are taught directly from the Bible. Until you get to know the Bible better, it will be difficult to discern other teachings that you hear.

So apply the Colossian message: Do not allow yourself to be taken captive by teaching with an unbiblical foundation.

As for Lee, just keep praying for him. As you have said, he sees that Jesus has strengthened your life. He may think that the famous actress' faith strengthens her, but he doesn't live with her. Keep letting your new life shine before him, and that will make more of an impact on him than any movie.

Your friend, Boston Paul

Dear Paul,

I put your Greek lesson to work this week, and impressed my neighbor. Charlie is a 68-year-old man who lives alone and seldom receives visitors. Yesterday after I picked up Andrew from school, I saw Charlie standing outside his door, so I stopped to talk with him.

For some time now, I had been feeling sorry for the man, thinking how alone he was. Anyway, as I was saying, I put your Greek lesson to use.

I was telling Charlie about my new faith in Christ when he told me that he was an agnostic. Well, I had gotten your letter the day before, so I knew about *gnosis*. I put the words together and figured out that an agnostic is somebody who doesn't know if God is there or not.

I didn't quite know where to go after making my brilliant discovery. When Charlie saw that I knew what an agnostic was, he seemed to realize that I wasn't just some bubbly religious fanatic. It seemed to make him want to talk with me.

So I just told him about the things that I have come
to believe in. I told him about how my parents had been
killed, and the various struggles I had experienced in
Boston. I shared about how I met you, Paul, in the laundromat. I told him that I believe God brought you and
me there at the same time so that my broken life could
be rebuilt.

After I shared about my life, Charlie just looked at
me, smiled, and said, "How do you know?"

At first, I didn't know what he was talking about.
Then he explained that a lot of people have had religious experiences that have seemed to help them. He
asked if I had seen the movie I told you about in my last
letter. He asked how I know that my beliefs are true,
and that the actress' are false.

I stammered out a few weak "becauses," but I didn't
have the answers. I knew he wasn't looking for an emotional testimony about the piecing back together of a
broken life. His "How do you know?" was from an academic standpoint. I didn't have much more to share
with him than my own testimony.

Charlie didn't cause me to doubt Christ, but I still
think I am lacking in my knowledge. Even if, as you say,
my experience is not lacking, I must be short somewhere in the theology department. I would have liked
to give Charlie some points about what I believe and
why I believe it.

On the bright side, he appreciated that I had
stopped to chat with him. He told me that he hadn't
had a conversation with anyone for a month.

Maybe Lee and I will have him over for dinner one
night. If I can't be the theologian he needs, perhaps at
least I can help take away some of his loneliness.
Heaven knows I can relate to him there.

I will wait again for your wise counsel. You should start charging me for all the time you take helping me grow. You have been a great long-distance friend.

Your L.A. Onesimus

Dear L.A. Onesimus,

S tart charging you?! I get enough of a charge from seeing you take your Christian life seriously. Believe me, I can relate to your problem this week. I remember some Jehovah's Witnesses coming to my door when I was a young Christian. I had thought that because I was now a Christian, I would automatically have the wisdom to convince them of their error. This assurance lasted for about five minutes. At that point, I realized that I could only convince them of my own ignorance. Rather than converting them, I had to make an excuse just to get rid of them.

So you feel like you are short in the theology department. Actually, because you are already a Christian, you do understand the basics of theology. Think about the day we met in the laundromat. You were a very broken person, and your sorrow seemed almost overwhelming. At that time, you certainly weren't thinking that all you needed to do was to learn some theology. But in fact, the message I presented to you is salvation theology. If we can remove your personal elements from it, we can analyze the theology that you actually learned.

The Gospel I shared with you that day in the laundromat contains two basic points. It is the same one the apostle Paul preached to his churches. These two points are the starting point of your Christian knowledge. They are the basics of salvation theology, the seed from which your faith must grow.

The first fact is that Christ died for your sins. The thing that distinguishes you from your husband Lee is that you have understood your sin problem. Now I think Lee is a fine husband, and a good provider for your family. I remember him telling me that he prays for business success. But the true Christian has come to agree with God's picture of their unredeemed selves. The Bible describes this state as "depravity."

In Ephesians, Paul said this to the Christians: "You were dead in your transgressions and sins, in which you used to live..." (Ephesians 2:1-2). This is interesting wording: we were dead in sin, yet we lived in it. As non-Christians, we were like walking dead people. Paul also reminded the Colossian church that they were once dead in their sins. This first point of salvation theology is very important to remember. Let me explain why.

Do you remember all the fuss raised a few years ago by that serial killer Ted Bundy? I heard that he had become a Christian as he sat on Death Row. At first, I had a hard time believing that. His murders would qualify him as one of the most hated criminals of the century. How could someone as wicked as Ted Bundy suddenly call himself a Christian during the final days of his life?

Then I thought about the apostle Paul. He lived during the first century, a time when men far more destructive than Ted Bundy flaunted their sin. During Paul's days, the mad emperor Nero would fasten people to the top of high poles and then set them ablaze to provide light for his lavish garden parties. Paul did not consider Nero to be the most evil of men. In fact, Paul confessed that he himself was the foremost of sinners.

If the Gallup poll had existed in the first century, few would have nominated Paul as the greatest sinner. But his confession teaches us something about the personal nature of sin. Understanding one's own depravity should make anyone the foremost of sinners in his own eyes. Having known myself for 78 years, I can say that I would give this title to myself without contest. After reflecting on this, I realized that my heart was every bit as wicked as Ted Bundy's.

This is the first point that you can explain to Charlie when the appropriate occasion arises. Illustrations abound about the sinful heart of man. You can see this fact in your two children, the people you have already met in Los Angeles, and most clearly, in yourself.

Because of our sin, we were subject to the wrath of a holy God. Christ's main purpose was to redeem us from our sin and its punishment. There are hundreds of religions and cults that consider Jesus a good teacher. But the early disciples, who heard Christ's teaching directly, mostly preached about His death and resurrection. This is called the priestly work of Christ. His chief mission in life was to shed His blood for man.

The second piece of knowledge that you must keep in mind is that Christ rose from the dead. If Jesus had remained in the grave, all that I have said so far would be theory. The world abounds with theories about God, which makes people like Charlie call themselves agnostics. They think that there is no way of knowing whether any of these theories is actually true.

The historical information about Christ's resurrection is reliable. Besides that, His resurrection appearances transformed the disciples from disappointed deserters to enthusiastic world-changers. After seeing the risen Jesus, they also mocked death through their bold witness, most to the point of martyrdom. They knew that death now held no power over them.

This same hope is built into Christians today. I recently spoke with a young mother of three who is suffering with brain cancer. She doesn't know if the doctor's treatments will remove the cancer. Nor does she know if God will heal her. Previously she had been an active woman, heavily involved in her church, her children's school, and being a homemaker. As the cancer now threatens to snuff out that life, she says that death is the least of her worries. A still confidence rules over her thoughts of death. The life inside her is as indestructible as Christ's own life.

These two points are the base of your spiritual life. These are the facts that you should share with Charlie. They are also the thoughts that you should reflect on regularly for your own spiritual well-being. The Colossians moved away from these basic points. They ended up with the appearance of spirituality, but not the substance of it. Since they abandoned the foundation of Christ, their own spirituality became false.

Now that I've finished explaining these points to you, I'll bet you would say that you already knew them. Am I right? You probably just needed time to think about what you believe, and for me to encourage you that you are on the right track.

I will pray for your friend, Charlie. Your desire to take away his loneliness will probably speak more loudly to him than any theological expertise you could offer.

Your friend, Paul

Dear Paul,

We had Charlie over for dinner. We spent the entire evening just talking about our families. Most of his family lives in this area, but they never come to see him. I think he appreciated the invitation. The subject of theology did not even come up.

I broke my first rule of church hunting: never find a church from the newspaper. It had been a few months since I'd even been to church. Lee is on the road again, so I thought last Sunday would be the opportunity to try again. To be honest, my visit to church did little more than confuse me.

This time, I chose the Spoken Word of Faith Center. Their newspaper ad claimed that they relied solely on the Word of God. Remembering your advice to stick with messages straight from the Bible, I immediately assumed that this would be the church for me to try.

The service was interesting, almost entertaining at times. At one point, the congregation even got to join in. We all stood up and shouted together (at the top of our voices), "I am a little god." Then we turned to the people around us, shook their hands, and told them that they are little gods. Of course this struck me as being odd, especially since Sunset had told me the same thing about herself. I assumed that these people had something different in mind.

The pastor suggested we repeat this phrase five times before we brush our teeth in the morning, and then five times after brushing them at night. This, he said, is assuming that we brush our teeth in front of a mirror. I don't know if this is something I should be doing or not. I can't imagine God having plaque.

Though the service was strange, I developed a certain respect for the pastor. He had an obvious speech impediment that caused him to add the "uh" sound to the end of most words. "Get" became "get-uh" and "money" became "money-uh." This problem increased as he became excited about things like that—getting money. Anyway, it was interesting to see how he could take his handicap and turn it into an advantage. Those annoying sounds actually added to the intensity of his message, kind of like a racing car's motor revving as it picks up speed.

Still, I didn't really feel at home at the Spoken Word of Faith Center. I felt like the people there had no problems. Maybe this church is the next step up, like graduating to the senior class. I still feel like a freshman.

The pastor said that even though you may not feel like a god, you must believe that it's true. For goodness' sake, I've had a hard enough time being human. Deity seems out of the question.

What is the difference between his beliefs and Sunset's? Their church claims to be based on the Bible. Does the Bible teach that we are gods? If it does, wouldn't you have told me that when you wrote to me about Sunset?

I snuck out of church just before the service was over. The parking lot was so full of Porsches and BMW's that I didn't want people to see me driving out in our old Volkswagen van. Maybe when Lee gets back from his trip, I can return to the Spoken Word of Faith Center in the company car.

Your L.A. Onesimus

Dear L.A. Onesimus,

Perhaps I should have warned you about the "little god" teachers earlier. I am certain that the pastor you heard differs from Sunset in his beliefs. Still, I believe that this message is dangerous, and can affect much more than the way we brush our teeth. This part of the church teaches that the moment we confessed Christ as our Savior, we became (like Jesus) little gods. The work of Christ becomes something like a spiritual photocopy machine, turning us out as mini-deities. I heard one such teacher describing salvation. He believed that Jesus is our prototype, and that we Christians are His genotype. According to this man, we have the genes of Jesus, and have been impregnated with His seed. As He was a deified man, so we can become little gods inside human skin.

Many of these teachers understand salvation differently than the historical Church. They believe Adam was originally created with a divine nature. When he sinned, our first father traded this for a satanic nature. Jesus then took on a satanic nature to redeem us and restore us back to our original possession of divinity. According to these teachers, we can exercise the same creative powers that God used to create the world. As God spoke the majestic Alps into Europe, so we have the authority to speak a new Porsche onto our driveway.

I believe these brethren mistakenly understand their salvation. But when we understand the awesome work of salvation done for us, and all the blessings we have received, one can understand how they come to their conclusions. Their mistake, though, is found partly in a faulty understanding of man. They have removed man from the finite realm.

The Colossian false teachers also attempted to discard their humanity. Gnostics thought that true spirituality meant leaving behind all the limitations of the physical body and the natural world. To them, the Christian life meant graduating from humanity into deity.

It would be helpful for you to consider Paul's word to the Colossian brethren:

For in Christ all the fullness of the Deity lives in bodily form, and you have been given fullness in Christ, who is the head over every power and authority (Colossians 2:9,10).

Gnostics used the word *fullness* as a catchword. Their thinking had them searching for supernatural experiences to help them achieve fullness. Paul told the Colossians that, in Jesus, they were given all they could want and need. They already had been made full in Christ.

Madeline, I have made a list for you of some of the things Scripture says you have in Christ:

1. Redemption from your old master, sin (Romans 3:24)

2. Peace with the God of the universe (Romans 5:1)

3. Forgiveness of every sin (Colossians 2:13)

4. Adoption by the only perfect Father (Ephesians 1:4,5)

5. Continual acceptance by God through Jesus (I Peter 2:5)

6. Justification (Romans 3:24)

7. Nearness to the Father (Ephesians 2:13)

8. Freedom from Satan's power (Colossians 1:13)

9. Great power in Jesus' name (John 14:12; Ephesians 1:19)

10. A Counselor, the Holy Spirit, who always fights for you (John 16:7,8)

11. An immovable foundation for life (Matthew 7:24-27)

12. Friendship with your Lord (John 15:14)

13. Holiness (I Peter 2:5)

14. A new family, the Church (Ephesians 2:19)

15. Abilities with which to serve your Father and His family (Romans 12:4-8)

16. New life and character (II Corinthians 5:17)

17. Comfort for all pain (II Corinthians 1:3,4)

18. The most sincere love (Romans 5:7,8)

19. A purpose for living (Ephesians 1:11,12)

20. Hope (Romans 8:22-24)

All these things are ours through Christ. This is part of the "fullness" that we have received through Him. You have been given everything you need through Jesus.

Consider the fact that "deity" did not make it onto the list. Be very careful of this teaching. True, we have been drawn into an eternal relationship with the Almighty God. Scripture teaches that Christ taught and enabled us to *know* God. He didn't teach us to *be* God.

In closing, let me say that your goal should not be to graduate to a church like the Spoken Word of Faith Center. The people there are no more spiritual than you. In fact, they are in danger of Colossian, false spirituality. You, like the useful Onesimus, are to see that your spirituality is in Christ. Build yourself up in Him.

If I looked into the mirror and thought I saw God there, it would certainly lower my opinion of Him. Especially since I take my teeth out to brush them!

Your friend, Paul

Dear Paul,

hanks for your lesson on deity. I read it through several times to make sure I understood it. And I have put the list on the fridge. I try to read it through a couple of times each day.

I've had some doubts about how well I qualify for some of the points. Lee has been gone a week longer than we had expected. It was a long separation, and yesterday I guess I reached the breaking point. I woke up in a foul mood, and started yelling at the kids for no reason. I think they were both wondering who the monster was that came out of their mother's room.

I had some shopping to do, so Joey and I took a trip to the supermarket. The rest of the town apparently had the same idea. Rain was coming down in buckets, and we had to park at the far end of the parking lot. By the time we made it into the store, we were soaked and shivering.

Anyway, the problem came when I was at the checkout. I had just seven items, so I went through the express line. Only people with fewer than nine items are allowed in that line. Well, the lady in front of me had at least 15 items. The line was long, but she finally made it to the cashier. I was fairly irritated by this time, and cold, wet Joey had begun to scream. I don't know if she noticed me looking back and forth from her cart to her face. I was somehow trying to show my displeasure.

Then, as the cashier rang up her purchase, the lady began to argue about the price of every single item. This was more than I could take. I began shouting at the woman right there in the check-out line. She and the cashier immediately stopped arguing and just looked at me. The people behind me must have thought I had completely lost it. I ranted for about 30 seconds (I think) and then burst into tears. I left my groceries in the cart, grabbed Joey, and ran out to the car.

I'm glad that I'm still a stranger here. I doubt that anyone in the supermarket would have known me. I came home, put Joey to bed, sat down for a good cry and then looked at your list. I felt none of those points were true about me. Sometimes I feel like I haven't changed, even though I now call myself a Christian.

Lee came home last night. I couldn't tell him about my outburst at the supermarket. I would hate to ruin my testimony in front of him. It's nice to have him home. I just wish it could have been a day earlier.

I don't really know why I'm writing this. I suppose I just want to get it off my chest. I know it's not the biggest deal in the world, but it certainly wasn't Christian conduct. If Geraldine Cabot had been present, I know that the demon brigade would be at my door now.

Your L.A. Onesimus

Dear L.A. Onesimus,

*T*he first thing I want to tell you is that the list is just as applicable after the supermarket incident as before. The ultimate question is not whether you feel you've changed. The truth is, through Christ, your legal standing before God has been changed.

The Colossians doubted their spirituality, and this

made them doubt their position before God. Paul wrote to them about the legality of their salvation in Colossians 2:11,12:

In him you were also circumcised, in the putting off of the sinful nature, not with a circumcision done by the hands of men but with the circumcision done by Christ, having been buried with him in baptism and raised with him through your faith in the power of God, who raised him from the dead.

You had a bad day. I agree that you blew it in the supermarket. But you know something? I can almost promise you that this won't be the last time you do something that's not very Christ like. If our position in Christ depends on whether or not we mess up, believe me, none of us would come even close to Him.

Paul told the Colossians that they had received an inner circumcision, a circumcision of the heart. Circumcision, an Old Testament ritual, parallels the New Testament rite of baptism. For the Jews, circumcision portrayed one's heart, open and devoted to God. Similarly, baptism for us symbolizes a heart submerged into Christ's death and raised with Him in resurrection.

Do you remember your baptism, Madeline? This rite only symbolized something that God had already done in your life. That something is called "justification."

Justification means publicly declaring the innocence of someone. Paul borrowed this legal word and applied it to the Christian. We were all spiritual criminals who deserved the death sentence. Jesus took this sentence upon Himself. Because of Jesus, God has declared us justified—innocent in the Father's eyes. Our justification is a legal decision made about us by the Judge of the Most Supreme Court.

Madeline, even though you did a less than hospitable thing in the supermarket, you did not alter your justification. God still sees you as an innocent lady, and He would gladly tell the whole world about your innocence.

If you think the word *justification* sounds theological and boring, you are in good company. I don't know when I last heard someone preach on the subject. But justification is actually the most exciting thing in the world. It represents our day in court, the time when we beat the eternal death sentence.

Imagine that you are a ten-year-old girl who burned down her parents' house while playing with matches. You are so ashamed you can't face your father. Then he seeks you out and says the magic words "That's okay, daughter." Only your dad could drive out the guilt and shame you would feel for burning down the house.

By declaring us justified, God has removed the shame of all the houses we have burned down. And we still tend to play with matches from time to time, doing the things we know we shouldn't. But this is the beauty of justification. With one decision, God has said that all past, present, and future sins are forgiven.

If God had been in that supermarket, He probably would have done three things. First, He might have rebuked you when you lost your temper. Then He would have somehow helped the lady in front of you solve her problem. Then He would have turned to the entire store and said, "This is my daughter Madeline. Isn't she great?" He would display your justification for the world.

About Lee, don't feel like you need to hide your imperfections from him. That would only amount to hypocrisy. Instead, let him know that you feel bad about the sins you commit. He will more easily see Christ in your humility than in your perfection.

Your friend, Paul

3

They Are More Perfect Than You

Dear Paul,

Thanks for the truckload of encouragement. I am still reading through the list. Point number three comforts me to no end: Through Christ, God has forgiven every single sin in my life. I am learning to understand God as a very forgiving person who doesn't bear grudges. His ability to forgive is certainly beyond my comprehension.

Speaking of forgiveness, Lee's brother Mike has been staying with us this week. We hadn't seen Mike for a few years. He was recently released from prison, where he had been doing time for stealing cars. You might say that Mike is the black sheep of the family. He and Lee are close in age, but have never been close as brothers. It was quite a shock when he showed up at our door.

The two brothers got into a heated argument the other night at dinner. They got loud, and Mike's language began getting rough. I thought they would start going at each other's throats, so I took the children out of the room.

You see, during Mike's time in prison, he had visited a prison counselor. This counselor boasted several years of education and experience as a psychologist. Apparently he has written a few books. Mike began visiting him as part of the prison requirement, but now actually feels that the counselor helped him a lot.

Basically, this counselor told Mike that he is not to blame for his mistakes. The reason Mike does the things he does is because he comes from a dysfunctional family. The psychologist pointed out several flaws in the way Mike's parents raised him, particularly his father. As Mike kept talking, it sounded like he was blaming his dad for his own crimes.

This was more than Lee could take. He blew his lid worse than I did in the supermarket last week. At least the whole town wasn't watching him, though. In a nutshell, he told Mike to get out of our house until he is ready to take responsibility for his own mistakes. Mike did, in fact, leave in a hurry. Lee has been brooding over that ever since.

What do you think, Paul? Is there any truth to the things that Mike has been taught? And what about taking responsibility for his mistakes? I have wondered about this in relation to my Christian faith. Is God's promise of forgiveness too easy? Will it only cause me to sin more?

I must confess that I'm happy to have Mike out of our house. I felt like I needed to lock everything up if I went out. Like they say, once a thief, always a thief.

On the bright side, I have another invitation to church next Sunday. One of the mothers at Andrew's school invited me to her church, the Perfected Saints of Holiness Assembly. It sounds to me like this may be a good place to learn about sin and forgiveness.

Your L.A. Onesimus

Dear L.A. Onesimus,

Lee's brother sounds like quite a character. It is often the ones who really enjoy their sin who try to unload the blame for it. Our culture, rife with modern psychology, often helps the sinner shift the blame for his sin. No, unless the heart of sin is dealt with, there can be no forgiveness.

The Church has also been guilty of treating sin too lightly. Some popular teachers say that our enemy is not sin so much as it is sin consciousness. The sinner is told that he must learn to view himself differently, to rid himself of his low self-esteem. The emphasis is then placed on forgiving oneself rather than on receiving and rejoicing in the forgiveness of God.

To correctly understand forgiveness, you must first understand the nature of sin. This should be easy for you, the mother of a small child. Scripture teaches that as Adam's descendants, we are born into sin. Perhaps your little Joey has started touching the TV buttons simply because he was told not to. He probably already knows how to break household laws, and he hasn't even had a teacher. I always say that the young ones are the best examples of both innocence and original sin.

Madeline, you will comprehend God's grace in forgiving your sin to the same extent that you understand your sin. Jesus once said to a self-righteous Pharisee that the one who is forgiven much, loves much. The Pharisee who had lost sight of his own sin could not receive such great forgiveness.

The Colossians, who liked to probe their own spirituality, needed Paul's reminder that God had forgiven them:

When you were dead in your sins and in the uncircumcision of your sinful nature, God made you alive with Christ. He forgave us all our sins, having canceled the written code, with its regulations, that was against us and that stood opposed to us; he took it away, nailing it to the cross (Colossians 2:13,14).

The Christian finds complete forgiveness through the Cross. Jesus already paid the price for our sin. Someone has said that forgiveness is free, but not cheap. The prison counselor did not champion forgiveness for Mike. He merely cheapened Mike's sin.

At the other extreme, Christians sometimes forget that Jesus paid for all their sin. During such times of forgetfulness, the Church has created systems intended to ensure the sinner's forgiveness.

A historial named Celano studied the life of St. Francis of Assisi. People usually think of St. Francis as the peaceful saint who loved nature. But Francis could be very strict with those in his charge. On one occasion, a secular person came to pray in the church which Francis was overseeing. He also left some money near the cross as an offering. Later, a brother picked up the money and placed it on the windowsill.

Francis heard about the brother's actions and became very upset. You see, the peace-loving saint considered money to be equal to dung. He rebuked the unsuspecting brother severely. As a punishment, Francis ordered the brother to lift the money from the window sill with his mouth and place it outside on a pile of dung, also using his mouth.

I am telling you this story to show you how a respected leader of the Church has viewed forgiveness. To Francis, repentance had to cost something before the sin could be forgiven. But the Gospel teaches that forgiveness is a free gift, accomplished completely by Christ's payment. God requires nothing from us but a sincere and sorrowful, "I am sorry."

This doesn't mean that we must confess every single sin in order to attain forgiveness. I remember attending a meeting that was filled with confession of sin. A few led the way, openly sharing some deep struggles they were encountering. Then the crowd came to the microphones in droves. People began confessing such trivial things as using someone else's pen without permission. A mentality had entered into the group, causing them to feel that public confession was necessary for forgiveness. What had begun with healthy openness degenerated into a silly game inspired by guilt.

The Bible teaches that we must confess our general problem of sin. You did this before me and the church here in Boston. For most Christians, this initial admission will result in humility, making confession a way of life. The genuine Christian has come to grips with his sin problem, and won't want to be tight-lipped about individual sins. He will confess them freely to God and to one another.

I noticed this humility in you when you wrote me about your blunder in the supermarket. God had forgiven you even before you committed that sin. But your letter to me showed that you took your sin very seriously.

And this answers your other question. No, I don't think that free forgiveness will lead one to take sin lightly. When we realize what our forgiveness cost Jesus, we will see sin in a very serious light. Your thoughts will focus on the goodness of God, and you will continually be amazed by His boundless mercy.

Let me just give your wrist a small slap for your final statement, "Once a thief, always a thief." The Gospel has power to change the thief into a kind person who gives freely to others. The power that can change Mike is the same power that has changed you. Mike will only be a thief at heart until Jesus changes him. Keep praying for him.

Your friend, Paul

Dear Paul,

Things definitely are not getting any better for me in my church search. I guess that I would rate my visit to the Perfected Saints of Holiness Assembly a disaster. I had no idea that Christians could be so diverse in the ways they worship.

I was invited to this church by June Graham, the mother of one of Andrew's classmates. We first met at a PTA function. I had listened in on a conversation she was having with a teacher that night. June spoke very openly about her Christian views, and wasn't afraid to disagree with the teacher's curriculum. Her zeal really impressed me. So I felt really encouraged when she invited me to church.

The encouragement lasted until I stepped foot inside the church. You see, the last time I had gone to church (the Spoken Word of Faith Center), most of the women were so made up that I looked like a street urchin next to them. This time I thought I would try to fit in a little better. I had my hair done, and decided to wear a touch more makeup than usual. The cherry red lipstick was a definite mistake. To my surprise and complete embarrassment, none of the women at the Perfected Saints of Holiness Assembly wore makeup. I noticed quite a few glares from the other women, and an occasional glance from some of the men.

June Graham didn't seemed flustered by my looks. In fact, my relationship with her didn't crash and burn until we had finished eating lunch at her place after church. I noticed that her husband didn't stick around very long after the meal. I hoped I hadn't said anything to drive him away. Anyway, June and I were having a pleasant chat over tea while the kids played in the next room. She was telling me about her recent victories over sin. She said that she hadn't sinned for four months. I was impressed, but not really surprised, since she did seem fairly perfect.

The problems began when Andrew came into the kitchen and asked for a drink of water. While June was getting it for him, he opened his little bag (he brings it everywhere) and pulled out his deck of cards. They had been a gift from Lee about a month ago. Not exactly the typical plaything for a nine year old, but they were special to him.

But by the way June shrieked, I expected to see an ax murderer walking through the door. She grabbed the cards from Andrew's hands and quickly threw them in the trash. A little flushed, she explained that it wasn't right for Christians to play with cards. I silently gulped down my embarrassment over the faux pas.

At that moment we heard a large crash from the living room, where the other kids were playing. By the time we got there, my little Joey was surrounded by pieces of glass and something that looked like the shell of a clock. After I yelled at Joey not to move, I apologized profusely to June.

Then it was my turn to be shocked. June was absolutely livid. The harsh words that poured out of her mouth (some of which I hadn't heard since college) were directed at little two-year-old Joey. He had broken a family heirloom, a clock June's grandmother had given her many years ago. The little guy took the rebuke pretty hard. I thought he would never stop crying.

June, on the other hand, needed only a few minutes to regain her composure and get back into the nice hostess role. But the clock wasn't the only thing broken. Her four-month string of perfection had obviously drawn to a close. I felt responsible for that.

From that point on, the visit was awkward, so I found an excuse to leave. On the way home I bought Joey, still sobbing, some candy as consolation. I also couldn't resist buying Andrew another pack of cards. It looks like neither June Graham nor myself are holy enough for the Holiness Assembly.

Your L.A. Onesimus

Dear L.A. Onesimus,

You have probably heard the old joke about the perfect person who had once thought he had made a mistake, but later discovered he had been wrong. It's a good thing June found out about her imperfection when she did. Without even knowing her, I have no doubts that those four months provided many opportunities for more reminders of her fallen self.

You have come into contact with a group that teaches absolute perfection. These people believe that the Christian's goal on earth is to grow into sinless perfection. Because different groups define sin differently, this perfection can also take on various forms. Some, like June, feel that playing cards is evil. These same people may also avoid movies, makeup, and music in their quest for perfection. One very extreme group in Church history even found clothing to be an obstacle to the original innocence of Adam. Called the Adamites, these people would attend church meetings in their birthday suits. Imagine the stares they would get at June's church.

Christians of most backgrounds search for spirituality as if it were at the end of a long, winding maze. They have used beliefs, methods, and activities as flashlights meant to lead them to their goal. They have a genuine desire to grow as Christians. This growth is called sanctification.

Sanctification means "the process or state of being set apart." The Bible teaches that sanctification is both a process and a state. First, we are sanctified through the work of Christ. We have been set apart as pure vessels, the property of a holy God. Second, we are becoming sanctified through the ongoing work of the Holy Spirit in our lives. In this second aspect of sanctification, we are growing as we rely on and obey the Lord.

June Graham desperately seeks to grow into moral perfection. In the annals of Church history, she is not

alone. Early one morning many years ago, a man
named Macarius sat in his small room in Alexandria,
Egypt. He didn't pay too much attention to the gnat circling his legs until it decided to take a chunk out of his
foot. Instinctively, Macarius brought a heavy hand upon
his foe. Smashing it to death, he saw that the gnat had
obliged itself to a final meal with his blood.

Macarius became upset with himself for killing this
hungry creature. He condemned himself to sit naked in
a mosquito-filled marsh for six months, attempting to literally have his remorseful flesh consumed. When it was
time to return home, Macarius had become so swollen
that some recognized him only by his voice. But as far as
he was concerned, he had won the victory over his flesh.

Both Macarius and June Graham understand sin incorrectly. The false teachers at Colossae thought that
people could be brought into sinless perfection
through denying their flesh. Paul pointed the Colossians back to the work already done for them in Christ:

*When you were dead in your sins and in the uncircumcision of
your sinful nature, God made you alive with Christ (Colossians 2:13).*

You see, the heresy at Colossae taught that the Christian should subdue his sinful nature by using rigid disci-
plines. Origen, the famous leader of an ancient
theological school in Egypt, made himself into a
eunuch so that he could teach female students without
temptation; an attempt to keep his flesh under control.

Origen inflicted major pain on himself, but he
failed to deal with the root of sin. Sin begins in the
heart. Here a great battle takes place between our sinful
nature and the Spirit of God. This sinful nature, Paul
told the Galatians, has been crucified along with its pas-
sions and desires. The crucifixion of our sinful nature

must become a reality to the Christian.

So the major weapon against sin is God's Spirit. I think that June Graham probably relies heavily on her own willpower to obtain sinlessness. As you witnessed, her will couldn't control a rash outburst of anger. Only the Spirit of God truly can tame an angry heart.

Madeline, do not be intimidated by such super-spirituality. In fact, it is not spirituality at all. When June Graham receives a true revelation of her own heart, she will be very disappointed. Only then can she grow into true sanctification. Then, she will cry out to her Redeemer to change her heart. After that, I would wager that her husband will not leave the table so quickly after lunch.

Your friend, Paul

Dear Paul,

*T*hanks for your advice about June. I sent her a note the other day, again apologizing for the broken clock, and offering to look at some antique stores for a replacement if she would let me know the make. But she sent back a note saying that it could never be replaced. I still feel bad, but it doesn't sound like she's going to forgive me very easily. Even though I've done everything I can, it's obviously not enough in her eyes.

I have had some more excitement (of the negative sort) this week with Andrew's asthma. I heard him wheezing the other night in bed. By the time I got to his room, he could hardly breathe, so Lee and I rushed him to the hospital. The doctors kept him there for two days, which was tough for him and for me. The poor kid has suffered so much with this problem.

Anyway, a few days later, I was watching a TV preacher. During one part of the show, he began speaking out different specific problems he thought his viewing audience was having. Most of these were physical problems. My heart leapt when he said that there was a child with asthma that God wanted to heal. He said that the parents needed to have faith that God was, at that moment, healing their son. Then I became very encouraged when he later reported about different ones who had phoned in to his show, testifying that God had healed just as the preacher had said.

I have been trying like crazy to have faith for Andrew's healing. Last night he began wheezing again, so I know that he isn't healed yet. But I really want him to get better. I somehow feel that it's all hinging on whether or not my faith is strong enough.

I told Lee about what the preacher on TV had said. He didn't take it too seriously, but I'm trying not to let that dampen my faith. The preacher said that if we have faith the size of a small seed, we can do anything.

I hope you remember to pray for Andrew, and especially for my faith. Somehow I think that your prayers might be answered a little more quickly than mine.

Your L.A. Onesimus

Dear L.A. Onesimus,

I will continue praying for your Andrew, and I hope that God chooses to heal him. I doubt that

God hears my prayers more quickly than yours. In fact, I would suppose that His ear is even more turned toward you, the agonizing mother, in this situation.

The Bible and my experience have taught me that God heals people today. When my own children have been sick, I have seen God instantly answer my prayer for healing. But you must learn, my dear Onesimus, that it is not one's faith that heals. God is the healer.

A few years ago, doctors told a close friend of mine that his cancer-stricken wife had only two months to live. Some faith-filled ministers dropped by their house and prophesied that the wife would be healed, and would live to the ripe old age of 120. The grieving young couple felt a glimmer of hope. They were told that if they could muster enough faith, God would certainly heal this illness. They tried feverishly. A few months later, the wife died, leaving the husband to grieve more than ever. Not only had he lost his wife, but the victory in healing he sought also slipped away.

I don't say this to discourage you as you hope for Andrew's healing. I am simply trying to point you to God rather than to your own faith. Misguided Colossian thinking wants to exalt ourselves as the key to victory. Instead we must exalt Christ as the key to victory.

This is much more than just a difference in semantics. One day when Jesus was walking along, a woman who had been sick for many years touched His garment and was healed. When He discovered who had touched Him, Jesus encouraged the woman by saying that her faith had made her well. But before she touched Him, she wasn't trying to work up her faith. In fact, she wasn't even thinking about her faith. All she wanted to do was to touch Jesus, the object of her faith. The story teaches that when we look to Jesus, we automatically have the faith needed to overcome.

But this faith is different from the one you wrote about. True faith in Jesus can stand through any disappointment, even the loss of a loved one. This is because the object of this faith, Jesus, never changes. This is the kind of faith the apostle John wrote about when he said, "This is the victory that has overcome the world, even our faith" (I John 5:4).

So, my Onesimus, remember the Colossian mistake and do not imitate it. Even though you desperately want to see your Andrew healed, keep your focus on Jesus rather than on yourself. He cares for your son much more than you do. And faith is something we have only when we don't look for it. It seems to disappear whenever we probe our own hearts in search of it. When we turn our gaze toward Christ, faith automatically fills us.

Your friend, Paul

Dear Paul,

Well, I can report that although Andrew is not yet healed, I am feeling much better. It has helped tremendously to take my eyes off myself and to look to Jesus. I still wish there was some way I could help the little guy. I continue to pray for him, but at this point that seems to help me more than him.

Charlie (the agnostic) dropped in the other morning. I had the TV turned on to that same preacher before he came, so it was blaring in the background as we drank coffee. The preacher was talking about the devil, which Charlie found interesting and even amusing.

The preacher talked about various spirits that afflict people. He said that he had recently cast the spirit of nicotine out of a smoker. That person, who had been addicted to cigarettes for many years, was able to quit smoking instantly. Another person had been afflicted with the spirit of karate. That one really made Charlie chuckle. The preacher went on to say that we Christians must take time to become more aware of Satan and his demons that are always trying to afflict us.

I switched off the TV, but Charlie's appetite for discussion had already been whetted. I had hoped more than anything that he wouldn't ask my opinion on this. Most of my knowledge on the subject has come via Geraldine Cabot, someone I wouldn't consider a very reliable source.

Anyway, I basically told Charlie that I didn't know. I said that the only thing I know for sure is that Christ died for me. The changes in my life since I have been a Christian prove to me the reality of Christ. But if he wanted to talk about the devil, he would need to find another Christian to talk to. At that point, he couldn't resist telling me that I am afflicted with the spirit of uncertainty.

Actually, though, Charlie appreciated my honest response. It didn't affect my testimony at all, or make him think less of my faith. He said that in this area, I am an agnostic like he is in the rest of life. I guess that's true in some ways.

All the same, I would like your input on this. How do I as a Christian relate to the devil? What kind of power does he have in my life? Is there anything to be afraid of? To be honest, apart from Geraldine Cabot's brief foray into my life, I haven't really considered the devil a whole lot. The preacher did say one interesting thing that made sense to me. He said that in order for any army to be successful in battle, they must know who their enemy is. Maybe it's time I learned some more about him.

For once I'm not asking your help because of a crisis or because of some strange theories I have formulated. So I hope this time there's nothing you need to correct me about. This alone makes me all the more expectant of your next letter.

Your L.A. Onesimus

Dear Onesimus,

I am so glad that you were honest with Charlie, rather than just agreeing with the TV preacher. So many Christians simply mimic popular teachers without taking the time to research ideas for themselves. I hope that you will do more than just pass along my ideas to him. Begin to search the Scriptures for yourself to learn what is taught about the devil. That is not intended as correction (so you needn't worry), but only as an exhortation.

The first thing you must know about your enemy is that he is already defeated. This is something that the Colossians also needed to realize. In his teaching to them about Christ's work, Paul said,

And having disarmed the powers and authorities, he made a public spectacle of them, triumphing over them by the cross (Colossians 2:15).

So, Madeline, through His death on the cross, Jesus defeated the devil. Unfortunately, even though he is defeated, the devil has not quit fighting against God and God's people. But no matter how he tempts us, we must always keep in mind that the devil is defeated.

Satan's goal is to destroy one's commitment to God. The Bible says that he pursues us like a lion stalking its prey. But the devil has only as much authority as God allows him to have. In the Old Testament story of Job, Satan initiated Job's pain, but could only do so with God's permission. As we see at the end of the story, God used Job's pain to teach him a great lesson. And so it is with most of Satan's evil plans for us. God helps us to either totally thwart the devil's schemes against us, or else God will use these to teach us wonderful things.

Sometimes Christians look for the devil so much that they seem to stop looking for God. This in itself can put the believer dangerously close to defeat. Paul told the super-spiritual Colossians that Jesus has disarmed the principalities and powers. Continual victory over the enemy comes by looking back to the work of Christ. We are not to focus on ourselves or on the battle. We are to lay hold of the Cross, the weapon of triumph. The devil can no longer hold us captive.

The TV preacher you heard was teaching on deliverance. He is one of those people who sees demons everywhere, and believes that demons are the cause of most sin. This sounds like Flip Wilson's comedic character Geraldine, who said the devil made her do it. Nowhere does the Bible teach that the devil makes us sin. He can tempt us, but the decision to sin is entirely our own.

I don't believe that the practice of deliverance is the norm for Christians. Still, there are some who suffer under certain demonic afflictions. I once taught at a Bible training program. One of the female students, a Christian for many years, suddenly became very depressed.

When the class began to pray for her, she began to speak in a low, inhuman voice. Obviously a demon was manifesting itself through her, similar to the things I had read in the gospels. Rather than hold a theological debate on whether or not demons could do this to Christians, the class banded together for their sister. In the name of Jesus, they cast out the evil spirit.

She was not "possessed" by the demon. Possession implies ownership, and we are owned by Christ, bought by His blood. Rather, somehow the enemy had gotten a particular foothold in her life. Some Christians need this ministry, but the Bible gives no indication that all or even most do.

The Bible does teach, however, that the devil does tempt every believer to sin. And this is his aim. He wants to destroy our relationship with God, our wholeness and happiness, by leading us to sin. At this point, we can again look to Jesus, confident that through His power we can say "no" to the devil.

Does it sound like I am saying the same things in all my letters? I am simply affirming the lordship of Jesus, like Paul did for the Colossians. Look to the One who has already defeated the enemy, and through Him you can do the same.

Your friend, Paul

4

They Have More Spiritual Experiences Than You

Dear Paul,

Happy Easter! Six months have passed since we moved to Los Angeles. I have gotten used to the smog and the traffic, but I still don't have any close friends. As for finding a church to be part of, I'm not sure how to proceed. After my initial experiences, I'm a bit paranoid about going to a new church.

Lee has been home more often these past few months, which is nice for all of us. The boys like having him around. I pray daily that he will become a Christian, though up to now, he has not seen the need. He is not opposed to my faith, he just feels it is something I needed during a time of depression.

Last night there was a news story about Easter celebrations in the Philippines. Several men had crucified themselves as a reminder of Christ's death on the cross. They didn't die, but their friends (?) actually pounded long nails through their hands and feet while they hung on crosses. It looked so painful. The reporter said that some actually submit themselves to this ritual each year.

Of course Lee thought they were crazy, intentionally receiving pain for no good reason and I tended to agree. But this morning, my Bible reading was from I Peter. I read in chapter four, verse one, "Therefore, since Christ suffered in his body, arm yourselves also with the same attitude, because he who has suffered in his body is done with sin." I saw a scriptural basis for the things they were doing. Maybe these men aren't as crazy as I first thought. Maybe they are far beyond me in terms of commitment to God and humility.

Are there any practical things that I should be doing to be humble before God and other people? I know that you're not going to ask me to literally crucify myself. Still, perhaps my beliefs should be more obvious to those around me.

For Lee's sake, I want to be careful about how fanatical I get. Right now he appreciates my beliefs. I would hate to freak him out by doing weird things.

Your L.A. Onesimus

Dear Onesimus,

 et me tell you an old, but true, story. Long ago in Syria, there lived a monk named

Daniel. During his younger years, when he received training in a monastery, Daniel visited another man named Simeon. Simeon lived alone on top of a stone pillar. Simeon's devotion to humble living had a profound impact on young Daniel. The younger man decided that he wanted Simeon as his mentor.

Daniel built his own platform atop two adjoining pillars. He remained at this address until he died 33 years later, descending only once to rebuke an emperor. Crowds flocked to hear Daniel teach and to have him pray for them. They considered him a spiritual giant for his great humility.

Do you get the point, Madeline? What I am saying through this story is that the concept of humility may be wrongly shaped through popular culture. The people of Daniel's day saw virtue in living in the most humble of places. In Asia, humility is comprised of self-effacing actions and words. If you were to tell a traditional Chinese mother that her baby is cute, she might respond by telling you that it is very ugly. She doesn't really believe her baby is ugly. Rather, her culture has taught her that such a statement is the humble thing to say.

Colossian humility was also based on external actions. To them, humility was a goal, something that they gloried in. In Colossians 2:18, Paul said to them,

Do not let anyone who delights in false humility...disqualify you for the prize.

Actually, the word *false* does not appear in the original language. The wording is actually, "Do not let anyone who delights in humility...disqualify you from the prize." This means that some people have wrongly made humility their goal. I believe that this was the mistake of the ones you saw crucify themselves in the Philippines.

When Paul wrote the church in Philippi about humility, he used Jesus as the example. He said that Jesus went to the cross as an act of service for us. Though He was God, He made Himself nothing in order to serve His creation. In this context, Paul told the church that true humility is to count others as better than themselves.

Humility is always relational. To be humble, we need another person to serve. The humble person doesn't seek a low status just for the sake of groveling. In fact, he doesn't want a position at all. His goal is the betterment of the other person, the one who is better than himself.

Let me give you a positive example. More than a hundred years ago, a missionary named Hudson Taylor left his home in Britain and journeyed to China. Though he had already given up home and family, he discovered that these sacrifices weren't enough to reach the Chinese people with the Gospel. In order to better serve them, he needed to give up his British appearance. He found a Chinese barber to shave his head, leaving enough hair to begin the long pigtail that was popular for Chinese men. He began dressing in traditional Chinese clothes that resembled pajamas. Other missionaries questioned Taylor's sanity. But Taylor deeply felt that any follower of the "lowly" Jesus would gladly abandon all in order to identify with the needy people of China.

In humility, Hudson Taylor considered the Chinese people as better than himself. This prompted him to sacrifice both family and culture. His actions weren't humility in themselves. Had he changed his dress like this while remaining in England, no one would have considered him humble.

My dear Onesimus, do not copy Colossian humility. You can be humble right now in your sphere of relationships. You are right about Lee. He is wise enough to see that there is no virtue in doing strange things for no reason. But if you continue to serve your husband, I guarantee that he will see Jesus in you.

A false concept of humility is just another mark of fake spirituality. Remember the Colossian mistake. They forgot that Jesus alone made them spiritual people. Humble acts of contrition were just another way that they sought a Christless brand of spirituality.

If I had time, space, and energy, I could write countless stories about Christians who have tried to be humble by doing demeaning things. But I think you get the point. Look to Jesus, the truly humble One, the One who gave up everything to serve you and me.

Your friend, Paul

Dear Paul,

Thanks for the advice on humility. I would apply it with my husband, but he left three days ago for a one-month sales trip. It was really tough to see him go this time. He's my only adult friend here in Los Angeles.

I really want to find a home church. I have started praying that I would find the right one. So far, I have tried three churches in Los Angeles, and I felt like a Martian in every one—completely out of place. Maybe I didn't give any of them enough of a chance. But I guess I'm just not that comfortable worshiping with people who think I am demon possessed.

How can I find the right church? I don't want to join up with a group of Colossians who will lead me down the garden path of deception. I want a church like yours in Boston.

I think I have learned through your letters that I should be very careful about the type of church I select. Many of them are mistaken in their view of Christ, correct? So where do I go from here?

Your L.A. Onesimus

Dear Onesimus,

*F*irst of all, let me explain that I believe God accepts people more quickly than we people do. I hope that my letters haven't caused you to be too wary of the Church. I do think that many churches have Colossian tendencies. Perhaps I have some myself. But Paul was quick to even affirm the Colossians as his brethren, people who were born of God.

So my point through these letters is not for you to avoid every Colossian you see. Rather, I want you to learn how to discern Colossian tendencies in yourself and in other Christians you meet. Observe the marks of false spirituality that can enter your life when you forget that Jesus has done everything for you. This is the message the Colossians needed to hear.

And no, most churches are not mistaken about the person and work of Christ. Many fail to continually affirm Jesus as their sufficiency, and then these ones often end up on tangents. That doesn't mean they are any less Christian than you or I.

As you are looking for a church, this is a good time to explain to you about various worship forms. Every church follows some pattern or form in their worship service. For some, this form may be very rigid, such as reading the same pages of the same book week after week. Other groups may be more free or spontaneous in their form.

I like to think of our church as a structured service with a charismatic influence. Our people follow the form of our denomination, but also appreciate a freedom to raise their hands, expressing themselves in worship as they sing. We also try to give opportunity for the Holy Spirit to bless the church through the members' gifts.

Madeline, varieties of worship services abound. I hope you are able to find one that suits you.

But the style of service is not the most important aspect of the church. The Church is people. In whatever church you choose, you will doubtless find that some people are difficult to love. Others will become your good friends. And there will probably be some Colossian spokes people, those who find that the church is never quite spiritual enough. They will be constantly thinking of various programs, methods, and teachings to correct this problem.

So I want to encourage you to find a group of Christians to fellowship with. Try to follow God in knowing which group you are to be committed to. Then once you have found them, jump in and enjoy the relationships that Christ has died for.

Your friend, Paul

Dear Paul,

I think I finally found a home church. The other day, while waiting for Andrew outside his school, I got into a conversation with another mother. Her name is Susan. As we talked, I discovered that she also is a Christian.

Susan immediately struck me as a warm and friendly person. We talked long after the kids were out of school, while they continued playing in the playground. I told her that I had been in Los Angeles for six months, but had not yet had any success finding a home church. She invited me to hers, named simply the Christian Fellowship.

I knew right away that Susan wasn't another June Graham type that would scare me off. And I immediately fell in love with the church when I went there on Sunday. The people all seemed very warm and friendly. No one eyed me suspiciously. No one seemed to care how I was dressed. It felt like home.

Susan also invited me to their mid-week cell group meeting, called a Care Group. This smaller group, I thought, would give me the chance to get to know some people. I went for the first time last night, and meeting these new friends was like a drink of cold water on a hot day in the desert. We worshiped, prayed, studied the Bible, and talked. I felt at home from the start.

But lest you think you are getting away with just hearing a positive report this week, I have another question for you. Two people in the home group were particularly vocal about visions they had seen. One of them said that he had a vision of Los Angeles being destroyed by an earthquake. I thought that was major news. Breaking up for coffee after that seemed a little awkward, if not inappropriate.

What am I to do about this vision? Should I believe the person (that I hardly know), or should I treat him like another Geraldine Cabot? The destruction of Los Angeles is not exactly trivial, and I would wonder why God chose to inform this person. But how do I know whether or not He did? I spoke about it with Susan after we left the house together. She said that she's learned not to believe every prophecy she hears. Then we parted company, and I'm left thinking about this prophecy of destruction.

I would like your input on this, before the next meeting. I would hate to see Los Angeles destroyed, especially since I've just made some friends here.

Your L.A. Onesimus

Dear Onesimus,

*Y*ou may be surprised to hear this, but that is not the first earthquake prophecy I have heard. A few years ago, a rather bold fellow prophesied that Vancouver, Canada would be destroyed by an earthquake on a certain day. The day passed without event, except that several naive people had fled the city.

Charismatics sometimes emphasize the experiential side of Christianity over the academic or the doctrinal side. The person who saw the vision of destruction is possibly seeking further experiences with God. Maybe he considers this to be truly spiritual Christianity.

It seems that our society at large is thirsting for more supernatural experiences. A few years ago, I heard about a woman in Hawaii who loved to go swimming with dolphins. She told how the dolphins freely shared their ideas, understanding, and teachings with her. They were the intelligent beings, instructing the woman in the mysteries of love and togetherness.

Of course this woman sounds odd, but she is not out of place in this generation. You saw the famous actress on television talking about her supernatural experiences. Psychic healing centers and hypnosis are becoming very common. There is definitely an increased interest in spirituality and supernatural phenomena.

The Colossians sought supernatural experiences as a quest for spirituality. Paul warned them:

Do not let anyone who delights in false humility and the worship of angels disqualify you for the prize. Such a person goes into great detail about what he has seen, and his unspiritual mind puffs him up with idle notions (Colossians 2:18).

They treated their own supernatural experiences with too much weight. This mistake caused them to lose sight of Christ.

Since God is Spirit, mysticism is an important part of the Christian life. History is full of mystics that most of the church has deemed orthodox. One of these is the well-known author Madame Guyon, who every year signed a marriage contract with Jesus.

Since you asked about the vision, let me give you a more general check list so you can evaluate supernatural phenomena yourself. I found these guidelines in a book I recently read by a man named Doug Murren. Test all spiritual manifestations with these points.

- Has experiencing this spiritual gift or manifestation taken your will from you? If so, it is not from God. I Corinthians 14:1-5

- Is it peaceful? Is this phenomenon palatable and intelligible to other spiritual people? If not, it may not be authentic. James 3:13-18

- Has this occurrence glorified God? Is Jesus the center of your experience, or are you the center? It is very clear from the Bible that Jesus expected that manifestations of the spiritual realm, as authorized by Him, would always keep Him at the center. All biblically sound spiritual occurrences are Christ-centered. I Corinthians 12:1-3; John 14-16

- Did this experience cause you to be respectful of others, or did it cause you to feel superior? If it caused you to feel spiritually above others, it was not an honest, legitimate manifestation. I Corinthians 14:1-5

- Are you willing to submit the expression of your experience to the scrutiny of your pastor and church leaders? If not, your experience would be suspect. I Corinthians 14

- Has this manifestation or insight strengthened your commitment to Christ, His Church, and the foundational truths of orthodox Christianity? No legitimate experience or gift will take you to the extremes or violate basic doctrine. Deuteronomy 18:9-22

- Has this experience caused you to be more concerned about others? If so, this experience is producing the kind of fruit that is biblical and legitimate. I Corinthians 12-14

- Has this spiritual event caused you to walk in harmony with Christ? If feelings of superiority and isolation occur as a result of your experience, it may not be valid.
  I Corinthians 12

- Is this experience open to anyone? If you feel that it is for you only, it is probably not legitimate or genuine, for God is no respecter of persons when it comes to spiritual experiences. Acts 10:34-36

My dear Onesimus, charismatic experiences have great value. The entire Bible is clear that supernatural living is part of being a Christian. Enjoy all of God's gifts. But test everything you hear, so that faulty experience does not lead you into deception.

At this point, I am not overly concerned about the future safety of Los Angeles. I look forward to receiving many more letters from my Onesimus out there in La-La Land.

Your friend, Paul

Dear Paul,

*T*hanks for the check list. I spoke with Susan about the vision, and she said that the guy who claimed to see it, Larry, is always seeing far-out visions. She said he has also prophesied several things about the future that have not come true.

Last night Susan couldn't make it to the Care Group meeting. She's the one I know best there, and is becoming a good friend to me. Anyway, since I have gone there for two weeks now, I thought I was familiar enough with the group to go without her. Now I kind of wished I hadn't done that.

We met at Larry's house this week. After the meeting, when most everyone was getting ready to leave, Larry and his wife asked if I would stay behind for a little while. I felt too new to decline. Another couple stayed, as well. Apparently all except me were "in the know" about why we were there after the meeting had finished.

We awkwardly tried to make conversation for a few moments before Larry got to the point. He finally asked if I had ever spoken in tongues. I said that no, I hadn't. They promised that I could do it that very evening if I wanted. So I was seated in a chair while the four of them gathered around and placed their hands on me. Then each of them began speaking in tongues. The only word I could make out was something that sounded like "shundolah," a sound I heard repeatedly from all four of them. They encouraged me to "let the language come." The two women even began rubbing my throat. It felt extremely awkward, the room was really hot, and I just wanted to go home. They prayed for at least half an hour before giving up. They all looked a little disappointed, and I somehow felt that I had let them down.

You have explained tongues to me in the past. I know that you speak in tongues, Pastor Paul. I don't feel as bad about not receiving this gift as I do about feeling out of place in the group I thought was home. This all just happened last night, so I haven't had a chance to discuss it with Susan yet.

Anyway, I won't quit attending the church or the Care Group because of this incident. I just need some perspective from Pastor Paul. And by the way, what does "shundolah" mean, anyway?

Your L.A. Onesimus

Dear Onesimus,

I don't think you need much counsel on this one. You seem to have a healthy perspective. God will give you the gift of tongues when He chooses to do that. Perhaps then you may find out what "shundolah" means. I cannot offer any insight on this mystery.

Do you remember that I once wrote to you saying the Colossian church had been affected by mystery religions? These mystery religions tended to consider that those with the greatest supernatural experiences were the superior people. Those who failed to receive such experiences were made to feel disqualified. Paul assured all the Colossians that Christ had already qualified them to share in the Kingdom.

Sometimes those in charismatic churches who have had great experiences try to force their experiences on other people. When the subject fails to duplicate the experience, he may feel inferior. This is Colossian Christianity, the tendency to exalt some in the church and to disqualify others.

Our English word *enthusiasm* comes from two Greek words: *en* and *theos*. Together, these two words mean "in God." In theology, this refers to the practice of religious ecstasy at the expense of sound doctrine. The Colossians fell into this error when they made too much out of supernatural phenomena.

of supernatural phenomena.

The Corinthian church also incorrectly emphasized the gifts of the Spirit. Paul wrote a longer letter to this church correcting their view of "charismata." The letter of I Corinthians gives us the most important role of spiritual gifts: to glorify Jesus. This is also the goal of our entire Christian lives.

When charismatic experience leads to someone's embarrassment, warning flags should go up. Even in my own church a few years ago, a leader surprised us all one day by asking a certain young couple to stand before the church. The elder went on to "prophesy" that this couple was having marriage problems. Even if the leader was correct, a public disclosure of this couple's marriage difficulties would not help their situation. The embarrassed pair never returned to the church after that.

I later used the situation to instruct the leader on the need to guard individual privacy. The goal of the Holy Spirit is not to embarrass the people of God, but to build them up.

My dear Onesimus, you are obviously growing in grace and in the Holy Spirit. Keep looking to Jesus, the one who has qualified you to share in the inheritance of the saints in the kingdom of light.

Your friend, Paul

5

But Do They Really Know Jesus?

Dear Paul,

I'm continuing to attend the Care Group. I told Susan about what happened the other week when Larry and company asked me to stay after class. She responded in a far different way than I expected. She laughed. They had done the same thing to her over three years ago.

This week I had a rather disconcerting experience. One day after the kids had gone to school and Lee had gone to the office, a smiling, middle-aged lady knocked at my door. She introduced herself as Rose, told me that she is a Jehovah's Witness, and said that she would appreciate just fifteen minutes to talk with me. I saw it as an opportunity to share Christ with her, so I invited her in. This was probably mistake number one.

Rose had brought a large, thick Bible with her. Believe me, in the end I felt very beaten up by it. Rose knew her stuff. She took me on a whirlwind tour through the Scriptures. I more or less sat speechless.

After she found out that I am a Christian, she mostly wanted to show me that Jesus is not God. Call me a slow learner, but I had very few answers to her arguments. The one that really got me was the passage she read from Colossians chapter one. I must have read that book a hundred times since you've been writing me. Could I not have noticed where it says that Jesus is "the firstborn of all creation"? It does go on to say that all other things were created by Him, but if He was created, then how can He be God? It seemed like Rose had a peculiar glint in her eye as she shared this one, like a lioness ready to pounce on her kill. I didn't let her know that I actually did feel like helpless prey.

When Rose saw that I was deflated, she asked me to make a decision. At this point, I realized that she had won and I had lost. So I brought our visit to an abrupt halt by saying that I needed to do something with my son. This wasn't a lie. I had promised Joey I would take him to the park sometime that day. This just happened to be the most appropriate time for me.

Before leaving the house, Rose gave me some pamphlets and urged me to make a decision soon. Boy, was I ever glad when I closed the door behind her. Of course I wasn't close to becoming a Jehovah's Witness. But as long as she remained in my house, I was reminded about how ignorant I am.

I remember you once saying that my heart obedience to Christ is more important than my head knowledge. My heart has no doubts about the truth of Christ. I think my life testifies to that well enough. But I am lacking in the theology department. Even if her theology is wrong, Rose knows the information well, and believes it with all her heart. What answer do you have for her point about Jesus being the firstborn of all creation?

At least this time I didn't try to discuss things about which I know little. I made that mistake with Sunset when I talked about hell. This time I heeded the advice of my mother, who would always say, "Keeping your mouth closed makes you look ignorant, but opening your mouth only proves it."

Your L.A. Onesimus

Dear Onesimus,

*I*f you're not sitting down, I would advise you to find a chair. This will most likely be a long letter. Madeline, a correct understanding of Jesus is the most essential foundation of our faith. Paul told the Corinthian church that Jesus is the only foundation that can be laid. In Ephesians, he said that Jesus is the Cornerstone.

To misunderstand the person and work of Christ is to place oneself on spiritual quicksand. Many cult teachers believe that Jesus was a good teacher and example, but not God.

Even in the Christian church, Jesus has been called a lot of things by different people. A different Jesus sometimes seems to be promoted for different occasions. He is sometimes pictured to be the great psychologist, the healer, the example, the buddy, the guide to success, the husband, the big brother, the source of wealth, and the positive thinker. I have even heard of surfers in California who refer to Jesus as their great Surfing Buddy.

In fact, most of these qualities can be attributed to the Jesus we serve. (I'm not sure about the Surfing Buddy, but I suppose that is something like a friend.) Though Jesus is all of these things, only one title stands out far above all others in Scripture. He is called Lord more often than anything else.

The word *Lord* means "master." It was a common term in the society of Paul's day. Slaves called their masters "Lord," and everyone gave the emperor this title. In the New Testament, Paul and other writers use this term almost exclusively for Jesus.

Jesus does call us His friends—if we do what He commands us. This means that we are friends of Christ only after we have made Him our Lord. Our view of His Lordship is the most important aspect of our ongoing relationship with Christ. Jesus is not like a friend that we go out with whenever we feel like it. He owns us. More than being the healer, buddy, or counselor who meets our physical and emotional needs, He is the one we bow before and serve.

In the Colossian church, problems of spiritual inferiority and superiority stemmed from this one mistake: The Colossians departed from the headship of Christ. This is the most basic and damaging mistake a Christian can make.

So, my Onesimus, cults are not the only ones who mistreat the person of Christ. The Church often loses sight of Jesus. Have you ever seen a chicken with its head chopped off? Its body hasn't received the message that it should be dead, so it runs here and there with no direction. This dying animal, jerking about with inconsistent spasms of life, is like the headless Church failing to keep Christ in His exalted place.

Since Rose stumped you with Colossians 1:15-20, let me show you some things from that Scripture. At this point, find your Bible and read those six verses. It is one of the most significant passages in the Bible about the person and work of Jesus. Observe how many times the word *all* is used. When a Christian learns about the all-sufficiency of Christ, he will no longer search for spiritual betterment outside of Christ.

There are several aspects of Jesus in this passage. I will list these for you after I discuss one in more detail. Rose told you that the phrase "firstborn of all creation" proves that Jesus is a created being, and therefore not God. I realize that this wording is difficult to understand. After all, in our twentieth-century American understanding, the word *firstborn* means the first child born to a set of parents, as Andrew is to you and Lee.

Thinking about Jesus as this kind of firstborn is to reduce Him to a big brother. In the heavenly hierarchy, He would be a step below the Father God that we worship and serve. Jehovah's Witnesses have come to this conclusion.

Immediately after Paul stated that Christ is the firstborn over all creation, he said that this same Christ created all things. It's a shame that you used Eileen's Bible to study this. The Jehovah's Witnesses have added the word *other* in their translation. Their Bible says that Jesus created all things other than Himself. This is not what Paul said. He said plainly that Jesus created all things. The very first verse of the Bible teaches that God created the heavens and the earth. This Jesus, then, was the creator God.

The word *firstborn* in this passage means "preeminence." Paul also taught here that Jesus was the first-born to rise from the dead. The Bible shows that He wasn't the first person to be physically resurrected. Two widow's sons and Lazarus beat Jesus to having that distinction. But there was a qualitative difference in Christ's resurrection. He didn't die again. His resurrection was the one that beat death once and for all, giving all who believe in Him the hope of eternity.

In the Old Testament, God's nation of Israel was called His "firstborn." This obviously refers to degree of importance, and not to the nation's age. Egypt was much older.

Jesus is the firstborn in importance. By His word, creation came into being. By His death and resurrection, fallen creation has been redeemed. He is the amazing God, worshiped by all Christians for His creative and redeeming power. We worship Him today, not just as a big brother or a buddy, but for being our God.

Madeline, the deity of Jesus is a cardinal point of our faith. This is often the point at which cults will stray. A part of the church which teaches that Christians are also gods is in danger at this point. By exalting themselves to the status of gods, they are closing the positional gap between themselves and Jesus. And He must always be the God that is exalted far above us, even though He is with us always.

Now let me list some other descriptions of Jesus from this passage. Using your Bible, see if you can find these descriptions of Christ:

- Jesus, the perfect image of God
- Jesus, the Lord of creation
- Jesus, the agent of reconciliation
- Jesus, the God/man

- Jesus, the prophet, the spokesperson for God
- Jesus, the priest, the Head of the church
- Jesus, the king, the ruler of all

Those Christians who truly understand the position of Christ will remain faithful to Him. When Chairman Mao was trying to stamp out the church in China, he closed churches, arrested pastors, and placed many in jail. A certain Pastor Ding was sent to a work camp far from his home. There the prison guards mocked him and the God that he served. "Our party," they said, "has destroyed your church. Where is your God now?"

Full of faith in Christ's Lordship, Pastor Ding refused to bow to the Communists. "You haven't destroyed the church," he replied. "You've only moved it inside these prison walls." The courageous pastor led several inmates to faith in Christ. He saw his Lord as the preeminent one, the firstborn of all creation.

You are doing well, my dear Onesimus. Don't feel too bad about being unable to answer Rose's arguments. You are certainly not the first Christian to lose an argument with a Jehovah's Witness.

Your friend, Paul

Dear Paul,

*T*hanks for taking the time to write such a long letter of explanation. Reading it did extend my mind, not because it was boring, but because I'm not used to thinking about such weighty things.

I know you must have spent a long time writing that

one, so I feel a little bad about asking for a further explanation. You see, one of the things you pointed out about Christ is the that He is the image of God. But Rose made this very point to show that Jesus was a part of creation. She referred me to a passage in Genesis, where it says that man was created in the image of God. She said that this also proves that Jesus was not God, because He, like man, was in the image of God.

So what does it mean when it says that Jesus is the image of God? I keep thinking of the pastor at the Spoken Word of Faith Center who encouraged his people to affirm their deity in front of the mirror every day. If Jesus is the image of God, and if I am the image of God, then I should be seeing God in the mirror, right?

On the home front, things are going well. I am really enjoying the Care Group, even though the visionaries still surprise me from time to time. The other week, one lady said she had a dream that someone in our group would become Governor of California. I looked around at the faces of everyone and decided she must have had too much pizza before bed that night.

Your L.A. Onesimus

Dear Onesimus,

I remember when my late wife, Gracie, was here with me. She sometimes saw the mirror as her worst enemy. To my eyes, she was the most beautiful woman on earth, but she sure didn't think so after a rough night. A true mirror will always tell the truth about us.

Jesus was a true mirror for the Godhead while on the earth. Paul told the Colossians that Jesus is the image of God. The word he used for *image* means "exact likeness." In Genesis we learn that Adam was created in God's image. This word means "resemblance." Jesus, far superior to Adam the man, displayed the Godhead through His body. This point about Jesus being the image of God shows both His humanity and His deity.

Madeline, don't search for God by gazing into the mirror. When Adam sinned, the image of God in man became distorted. It was still possible to see God in people's lives, but only in a fragmented way. It would be similar to seeing bits of one's own reflection here and there in the shattered ruins of a broken mirror. Christ, however, was the perfect image of God. And Christians now bear God's image in a better way because that image (Christ) lives within us.

It is often difficult to see God's image in ourselves. When we look into the mirror of God's standards, we can easily see our unkempt morals and disheveled attitudes. At these times we must learn to look to Christ, the perfect image of God.

I once knew a young woman filled with guilt over her immoral past. She couldn't forget the sinful things she had done and still wanted to do. One day as she read her Bible, God opened her eyes. She saw that Jesus had once and for all done a perfect work in her. Jesus had taken the shattered bits of God's image inside her and had placed the whole mirror of Himself in her life. From that day on, she was able to walk in a new purity, reflecting God to those around her.

Our faith, values, strength, and character are all distorted this side of heaven. Giving God the broken pieces of our humanity is like trying to sell a smashed mirror at a garage sale. Only Christ, the perfect image of God, is able to restore us. As we rely on Him, we are filled with the image of God.

I'm glad you are enjoying the Care Group, and that you're learning to weigh the prophecies of the Colossian sector. I agree with your conclusion. Zealous Christians sometimes get mixed up between intuition of the Spirit and intuition of rich food.

Your friend, Paul

Dear Paul,

I know that I am extremely slow, but please, just give me one more explanation. If I meet another Jehovah's Witness, I will need to know what I'm talking about.

What does it mean that Jesus was both God and man? You said in your last letter that the point about Jesus being the image of God referred to both His humanity and His deity. I think I can understand one or the other of these—either His humanity or His deity—but not both at the same time. Are we talking about percentages? Like, was He 75 percent God and 25 percent man?

I'm sorry for taking so much of your time with this. I brought up this question at the Care Group, but nobody really had a good answer. Most of them said they had never thought of it before.

I am beginning to realize that a lot of Christians don't know that much about what they believe. I feel like most of my personal struggles are subsiding, and that I am wanting to grow more in knowledge. I hope this desire is okay, and not unchristian in any way.

Actually, Susan and I have been reading your letters together and studying Colossians. So the question in this letter is actually from both of us.

Your L.A. Onesimus

Dear Onesimus,

*Y*our desire to grow in knowledge is a godly desire, as long as the knowledge of Christ is your chief goal. Remember the Colossian mistake regarding knowledge. Their goal was to understand the deep mysteries so they would be seen as the most spiritually illumined.

The question you have put to me is also a very deep mystery. Francis Schaeffer said that there are two major paradoxes in Church history. The first is a hotly debated piece of theology—God's sovereignty and man's responsibility. The second paradox is the fact that Jesus Christ was at once complete God and complete man. So if you want to talk percentages, then Jesus was 100 percent of both.

Speculation over this concept has produced strange teaching in cults and even in the Church. Some gnostics—the same false teaching of Colossae—believed that Jesus' body was a shell which was being used by some divine presence. The more extreme form of this thinking taught that the man Jesus developed into deity. This is similar to the Christ-consciousness that some of today's cults think we can obtain. This is what Sunset believed.

Paul described Jesus as being both human and di⁻

vine. He told the Colossians that the fullness of God
dwelt in Christ. Other New Testament writers described
Jesus as the "I am" of the Old Testament. This was a
unique name for God. I once heard a preacher teaching his flock to claim this "I am" phrase for themselves,
and in the same way declare their own deity. But in the
Bible, God reserves this title for Himself.

Though He was divine, Jesus also suffered as a man.
He even allowed His creation to abuse Him as a disliked
man. He walked in our dimension of physical nature in
order to suffer and die for us. Moreover, He modeled
true humanity for us. He told stories like that of the
Good Samaritan to explain what it means to be a righteous person. He reached out to those who had been
most neglected by other humans.

Madeline, you will not completely grasp the concept
of Jesus being fully God and fully man. This is a teaching of Scripture that is true even though our finite
minds are unable to ponder its depths.

But this truth has a profound application. In Hebrews we see that Jesus is a human high priest who can
sympathize with our weaknesses. In the same book, we
also learn that He is the eternal high priest, reigning forever from heaven. That is our Lord. He became a person, and can relate to our struggles. He is God, and can
help us overcome our struggles.

My, what a change I can see in my Onesimus! Eight
months ago you were wanting to scale a ledge in Los Angeles. Now you are deeply in love with your Lord, wanting to understand the depths of His person. Perhaps I
shall be writing to you for advice soon.

Your friend, Paul

6

The Mystery of Christ

Dear Paul,

*T*hanks for the encouragement about the changes you have observed in my life. Yes, I do think I am growing as a Christian. And I have even begun to feel content in Los Angeles, a place I once thought I could never consider home.

I can't put into words how much your letters have helped me. At times they were like a map out of the woods when I felt very lost. But as for your last comment, I don't think your work is finished yet. If I were you, I wouldn't place any money on the possibility of me sending you advice.

In your letters you have mentioned the concept of mystery a few times. This week at Care Group, Larry (our visionary) gave a book to each of us. The book is titled *Unraveling the Revelation and Mastering the Mystery*. It is written by the pastor of a church called the Sanctuary of the Seven Thunders. He claims he is the final prophet before Christ comes.

I hadn't read much in the past year except for the Bible and your letters. But since Larry had gone to the expense of buying me a book, I thought the least I could do was read it. Now that I have read it, I have a question for you. But first let me explain to you the basic thrust of the book.

I think I have learned enough through your letters to identify this author as a Colossian. He relies heavily on revelation knowledge. In fact, he has even built something in his church called the Revelation Chamber, a special office where he spends his time praying and writing. Here he gets visions and revelations, some of these for the purpose of explaining the Bible, and some to explain his own role in what he calls, "these last days."

He claims that God has explained the book of Revelation to him. (I haven't dared to read that book yet.) It contains some mysteries that he says no one has understood yet. But, he claims he was told the meaning of these mysteries while in the Revelation Chamber. His explanations had something to do with thunders, seals, and a silence in heaven. He lost me at this point. I did understand, however, that he feels he is the one sent to break heaven's silence to the world.

I suppose it would be easy just to discount the man as a Colossian loonie. But he also includes in the book several stories about how he's healed people and cast out demons. His power stories sound reminiscent of Christ's miracles in the gospels.

My question to you is this: Don't these miracles confirm the man's credibility? How could his teaching and personal claims be false if he has done so many mighty, supernatural works? I remember reading in the Bible that Jesus did the same thing when John the Baptist asked if He was really the Messiah. Jesus sent word to John about the mighty deeds He had done.

From the way Larry talks, I get the idea that he would like to move to Chicago just to be in this guy's church. I think I realize that the Colossian heritage is firmly implanted in both Larry and this author. But how can I cast such a judgment on the author when he has done so many mighty works?

I guess I still lack the ability to analyze the book. So I will suspend final judgment on this one until I hear back from you. Are there any guidelines that will help me know whether or not his claims are true?

I know that you're more of a spiritual Agatha Christie than I am. You always have a way of figuring out mysteries and mysterious people.

Your L.A. Onesimus

Dear L.A. Onesimus,

*Y*ou have come across a real doozie this time. I am extremely pleased that you are able to recognize a Colossian when you see one. The author you spoke of probably fits the bill perfectly for a Colossian tangent.

Maybe I haven't explained the concept of mystery very well yet. I did mention to you that in the Bible, the word mystery does not mean "mysterious." The Chris-

doesn't have to be Agatha Christie or Sherlock Holmes before he can understand the deepest implications of Christianity. As I said before, the mystery is not meant to befuddle, but simply to cause us to worship God. We stand in awe, mystified that the God who created us would consent to live like us and in us.

Paul said to the Colossians that "the mystery has been kept hidden for ages and generations, but is now disclosed to the saints" (1:26). In his next sentence, he said that "God has chosen to make known among the Gentiles the glorious riches of this mystery, which is Christ in you, the hope of glory." Madeline, this is the mystery that the New Testament says is already revealed to us: the fact that Christ lives in and among us.

Once when Jesus prayed, He thanked the Father that "these things" were hidden from the wise and intelligent, but revealed to babes. At the time, He was referring to His disciples, the uneducated "babes" that followed him. The pompous legalists bent on external glory were the epitome of the world's wisdom and intelligence.

Today you and I are the "babes." We have received Christ as our Lord, and rely on His Spirit to lead us. Some things remain mysteries to us, things that we might not understand until heaven. Our goal, then, is to be built up in Him, to really know Christ. The most spiritual Christian is not the one who knows more tricks than anyone else. The spiritual Christian is the one who understands the sufficiency of Christ's life, then patterns his own life accordingly.

My dear Onesimus, Christian maturity does not depend on mystique. The Christian, regardless of whether or not he's a church leader, does not need a revelation chamber so that heaven can beam messages down to him. He must simply walk with the Lord Jesus, surrendering all of his life to Him.

Paul told the Colossians that he strove to maintain the Lordship of Christ in his life. He worked hard to keep Christ central. When he had a great vision, he needed a reminder of his own weakness so that he would continue to depend on Jesus for everything.

The supernatural works claimed by that author could have several explanations. Jesus said that not everyone who does great miracles is even a Christian. Apparently the devil can counterfeit miracles.

Also, the Bible draws no connection between miracles and wisdom or maturity. Perhaps that author does do miracles by the power of Jesus. That doesn't mean his theology or his revelations are correct. Supernatural power does not equal perfection or even wisdom.

Let me just ask you one question about the book you read. How much did the author talk about Jesus and the Cross? This is often the acid test in discerning truth. Heaven did not break its silence by sending this man some revelations. The Bible says that Jesus is God's message to the world in these last days. If the book was low in Jesus content, then the author probably wasn't speaking for heaven at all.

Most people, ministers included, like to talk about themselves. I once heard of a pastor who boasted that he had authority over 12,000 people. He spent more time certifying his position than he does exalting Christ. Sadly, this is done every day by ministers around the world.

So, Madeline, take some time to analyze the content of your own conversations. How great a role does Jesus play in your speech? We really do discuss the things that are most important to us. How much does your Care

Group talk about Jesus?

I hope that your friend Larry doesn't move to Chicago just for the sake of being with this pastor. It is true that Colossians often stick together. But I should think that he could find many in Los Angeles.

Your friend, Paul

———————

Dear Paul,

I am encouraged that it's becoming easier for me to spot a Colossian and Colossian tendencies. I guess the author of *Revealing Revelations and Mastering the Mystery* was fairly obvious, especially since Larry gave me the book.

This week I attended a seminar on stress-free living. I don't normally attend seminars (in fact, I don't ever remember attending one), but Susan was already signed up and she had an extra ticket. Her husband had been planning to go with her, but he ended up having to attend a company function. The topic of the seminar was, very simply, "How to Live Without Stress."

Susan has been under quite a bit of pressure these days. She comes from a painful family background, and grew up with a lot of bickering. She still isn't very close to her family, especially since they all live in Florida. But she's happy that there is a bit of a distance between them now.

Last week her parents phoned and said they were coming out to Los Angeles for a visit at the end of the month. Susan has been climbing the walls with worry ever since. She envisions a non-stop verbal fight from the time they come to the time they leave. She dreaded the thought of dragging her husband and kids into World War Three. So she was hoping this seminar would give her some keys for how to go through this time without stress.

I came home from the seminar feeling very relaxed. They showed us some breathing exercises that we could do when feeling under pressure. They also taught about finding a quiet place and learning to focus, reevaluating the stressful situation.

A lot of the teaching made sense. I especially hope that it comes in handy for Susan.

Have you ever attended a seminar like this? I think the tickets were quite expensive. Isn't this kind of stress-free living a good goal for Christians, too? I mean, Jesus did say that Christians would have peace, right?

So, my teacher, since you did suggest that I would be giving you advice one day, here's my first piece. When you have a tough day, find a quiet place, then breath in and out until you feel yourself beginning to re-lax. Try to imagine all your troubles being expelled with the wind of your breath.

Your L.A. Onesimus

Dear Onesimus,

*T*hanks for the advice, but in all humility, I think I will pass on it. It's true that Jesus did call us to peace, but He said that we would have peace in Him, not through breathing exercises. I think I'll stick with His promise rather than embrace techniques from an expensive seminar.

Self-help seminars have bombarded our North American society, including the church. There are seminars that teach how to be completely successful, how not to be co-dependent even though your entire family is dysfunctional, how to have the confidence you always wanted, and how to be totally free from sickness. And with the seminar that you just attended, you can learn how to do all these things without stress.

I hope you realize, Madeline, that I'm not really belittling these things. God wants good things for His children, and sometimes seminars like these are a genuine help. But the Christian who depends on self-help seminars is in danger of Christless Christianity. Sometimes it seems that Christians even substitute these techniques for Jesus himself.

Madeline, there is no shortcut to abiding with Christ. Paul told the straying Colossians, who were departing from Jesus, that "just as you received Christ Jesus as Lord, continue to live in him, rooted and built up in him, strengthened in the faith as you were taught, and overflowing with thankfulness" (Colossians 2:6,7).

So this week I want you to ask yourself a question about the seminar you attended: Does the teaching you received assume that one's heart can be at peace even without Christ? In other words, would the effect of the seminar be as great for a non-Christian as it would be for a Christian?

Be very careful of substituting a technique for Jesus. For Susan, Jesus Himself will heal her heart of past family hurts. This is the application of the letter Paul wrote to Colossians. As her sister in Christ, encourage her not to seek fullness outside of Jesus.

Sorry to snuff out your first piece of advice to me.

Please don't be daunted. I am always open to learning, if Jesus is the goal.

Your friend, Paul

Dear Paul,

Thanks for the advice on the seminar, even if it did constitute a mild rebuke. The breathing exercises only lasted a few days for me. I came down with a major cold last week, and had trouble breathing at all.

We had some dissension in the Care Group this week. Larry asked everyone what they thought about the book he had given us. I think several of us just stared at the floor after he asked the question. We didn't want to make eye contact with him.

Well, since nobody answered Larry, he launched into a lengthy talk about how the book had given him so many new perspectives. He told about some of the things he had decided to do in light of the last days, which, by the way, the book claimed would be within the next three years. Larry and his wife are considering selling their house and sinking the money into the author's ministry. Actually, I'm pretty sure that this is Larry's desire more than his wife's.

Jim, our home group leader, is extremely tolerant. He just let Larry talk without interruption and without correction. I thought for a minute that Jim must have agreed with Larry from the way he kept nodding his head as Larry spoke.

Finally, Susan couldn't stand it any longer. She spoke up and shared some of the thoughts from your letter. Larry seemed to take her opposition personally. He began defending himself, saying that he had spent a lot of time in prayer as he read the book. It became clear that the rest of the group had opinions on the subject, as well. Some thought that this man's teaching is very valid. They thought his miracles confirmed that. A full-scale disagreement began, and we spent the rest of the evening arguing over this book. I was glad to see that Jim, the leader, did not agree with the author's "new revelations."

I left the Care Group that night feeling like our hearts were more angry than caring for each other. Larry seemed surprised that some disagreed with him, and left without saying goodbye to anyone. Susan felt like she started the whole argument, though she still thinks that something needed to be said.

We are feeling a little nervous about next week's meeting. I hope that the group can get over this hump. This week when it came time to pray for each other's needs, the only one who prayed out was Jim. He seemed a little deflated about that, too. Any advice on how we can rectify the situation? Should we give Larry the boot?

Your L.A. Onesimus

Dear Onesimus,

So you have discovered that your Care Group is not perfect. This would have become evident sooner or later. Let me explain the basic reason why Christian unity often breaks down.

I remember one of the first churches I ever pastored. When I first came there, I quickly realized that the youth choir was an important part of the church life. The church loved this choir, and treated it like a showpiece. To me it seemed that no matter what changes my leadership would bring to the church, I had no freedom to change anything about the youth choir.

It wasn't until I became acquainted with some of the kids in the choir that I began to see problems. Some of them were involved in immoral relationships, and many reeked of pride. I made a decision to put the choir on hold until some of these problems could be dealt with.

How do you think the church responded? With the departure of the youth choir, the church had suddenly lost its identity. A lot of people were mad at us in those days. Quite a few just up and left, moved on to other churches. Apparently the choir had become the basis for that church's unity.

Larry is asking your Care Group to become unified around the message of a certain book. But a difference of opinion should not cut the bonds of the Spirit. Your unity is not found in a mystic who receives visions in his revelation chamber. Unity is found in Christ alone.

Once the Colossians had dethroned Jesus, they had ceased recognizing Him as the head of the church body. Paul wrote that his purpose for them was that their hearts would be united in love, so that "they may have the full riches of complete understanding, in order that they may know the mystery of God, namely Christ" (2:2). He also told the Colossians that Jesus had made peace by the blood of His Cross. As their members sought things other than Christ, their unity would be threatened.

In Ephesians, Paul said that Jesus had broken down the dividing wall of hostility. There are two things that can stand between Christians: the person of Jesus or a dividing wall. Jesus joins people together like a bridge, but the self-erected wall separates. I believe that if Christians attempt to find unity in something other than Jesus, that thing will eventually become a dividing wall.

If your Care Group insists on building relationships on the basis of books or visions, everyone will be disappointed. It would be only a matter of time until every one of you found something trivial to disagree over. I don't say this because I think you are trivial people. I am giving this warning because I assume you are all human beings.

Madeline, if I had a spry hand and a few hundred pages of paper, I would list some of the many things that have divided churches. I heard of one family who left a church because someone took the father's designated coat hanger in the church foyer. In other words, his unity with that group of Christians depended on a thin piece of metal.

If all Christians honestly examined their church relationships, I am sure they would find that many reasons for unity are equally as thin. Disputable points of doctrine, programs, experience, methods—we often use these as points of reference for unity. For many Christians, these very things just as often become dividing walls of hostility.

It is impossible for Jesus to divide two people who each love Him most. My exhortation to you is to lift up Jesus in the Care Group. Don't even talk about the book—you don't need to criticize or affirm its contents. It doesn't sound like everyone can discuss it objectively at this point. Rather, seek to draw the group back to looking at Jesus, the One who died for their relationships.

By no means should the group kick Larry out. Let him know that you care for him as a brother in Christ. I think that as you do this, he will also begin to care less about his Colossian tangents and more for Jesus.

Your friend, Paul

Dear Paul,

I swallowed hard after reading your letter. It struck me as being very right, and my first thought was that I need to take action. I received it on Thursday morning, and the Care Group meeting was planned for that evening. Believe me, I prayed all day that I could say the right thing in the Care Group. I felt like I was getting ready to preach a sermon.

Well, as it turned out, I didn't have to say anything. Larry opened the meeting by apologizing for making too big a deal out of the book. He said that when he and his wife got to the car at the end of last week's meeting, she said that she agreed with Susan. She didn't want to sell their things for the sake of this man's ministry. This was the first time she had felt the courage to disagree with her husband on a spiritual issue.

At first Larry had taken this pretty hard, but he thought about it for a few days. You know, it almost seemed that you sent the same letter to him that you did to me. He saw that he was placing something above Jesus in his life. He apologized to the group for doing this.

Jim had prepared a message on unity that evening, but never gave it. We practiced unity instead, and spent the whole evening praying for each other. I guess we had to make up for last week, too.

Changing the subject, Susan's family has come and gone. In the long run, she didn't feel that the stress-free seminar helped her handle her stress. As she expected, her family did end up arguing most of the time. Her parents are not Christians, and they spent a lot of the time arguing about Christianity. Poor Susan is feeling tired and discouraged, but relieved that they are gone. I think it is so sad that she feels relieved about not seeing her parents for a long while.

I'm not sure how to help Susan in this situation. We prayed for her and her husband at the Care Group, but I wish there was something more I could do.

Your L.A. Onesimus

Dear L.A. Onesimus,

I'm glad that things worked out for you in the Care Group, though I'm sorry you missed your preaching debut. Jesus sometimes preaches the message to our hearts without the use of a human vessel. This was the case with Larry.

About your friend Susan, the only thing you can do for her right now is to pray. Discouragement creeps into our lives because of misplaced or unrealistic expectations. For example, if I had given myself the goal of seeing my church grow to 100,000, I would be a very discouraged man right now.

The apostle Paul encouraged the Colossians to continue to live in Christ, "rooted and built up in him, strengthened in the faith..." (2:7). Strength comes through simple, steadfast faith in Jesus. If our gaze is on Christ, discouragement will not affect us.

When I was a young minister, I longed for God to heal people when I prayed for them. I seldom saw this happen, and began to feel very discouraged about it. I blamed myself, my prayer life, my lack of sanctification, and anything else I could think of. Instead of looking to Jesus, I began to look at myself. You see, I wanted to be the perfect minister (and I had my own ideas of what the perfect minister should be), and I wasn't attaining that goal. A wise author named Francis Schaeffer once said that if the perfectionist doesn't attain perfection, then he feels he attains nothing at all.

Encourage Susan with the fact that she and her family are not perfect. Difficulties are a part of life, and they are not totally erased when we become Christians. She doesn't need to pray that God would take away her difficulties as much as she needs to ask Him to give her the right perspective. If she can see Jesus in this situation, her discouragement will be dealt a death blow.

I am not a psychologist, so I have nothing more to offer Susan than the simple biblical perspective I have just shared. She will know God has done this if she feels joy rather than sorrow the next time her parents plan a visit.

Your friend, Paul

7

How Spiritual People Relate to the World

Dear Paul,

One of the things that makes Susan's family situation so sad for me is that I miss my own parents so much. I would give almost anything for them to be alive again. I can't relate to the joy Susan said she felt when her parents said goodbye at the airport.

These days I'm feeling resentful about Lee's schedule. The end of the year sales bonus is coming up next month. All the salesmen with high amounts of sales get a bonus, with the highest bonus given to the ones who are salesmen of the year for their region. Lee should get the basic bonus without a problem, but for the last while, he has been pushing himself like crazy to be salesman of the year. I think I have seen the garbage collectors more than I have seen my husband in the last six weeks.

On one of Lee's rare evenings at home, I tried to talk with him about it. He had been working the calculator at his desk, so I knew that my presence would be a distraction. Anyway, I told him that I really didn't like him being gone so much, and then I began to cry. Of course, this was certainly not the first time Lee had seen me cry, but this time his response was different. Rather than becoming empathetic, he just got mad. He said that I didn't understand that he was working hard for me and the kids. He thought that I was being totally ungrateful for all his hard work. But now that he knows I would rather have him home, he still hasn't changed anything.

Anyway, I'm not writing for advice on that. I shared our struggle at the Care Group, and they prayed for me. But then a guy named Phil (a friend of Larry's) told us his story. He had been a driven workaholic for many years until he felt that God asked him to quit his job. He did that two years ago, and hasn't worked since. Now all Phil does is pray and live on social benefits.

Phil said that if Lee ever gets saved, he's going to need to make some drastic changes in his attitude toward work and life. He said that Lee should take a year or two off work just to pray and go on spiritual retreats. He said that Lee needs to get the world out of his mind.

I know that Phil's solution sounds spiritual, and even a little noble, but I'm not comfortable with it. I don't know why, but I guess deep down I would rather have a husband with Lee's work ethic than Phil's.

Is there any truth in Phil's advice? His wife was sitting beside him as he shared his view on this. I watched to see her nods of approval, but she mostly just looked down while he talked. Maybe she's not convinced, either.

Your L.A. Onesimus

Dear Onesimus,

Thanks for not asking advice regarding you and Lee. I have a feeling God will work that out Himself in a way that doesn't need my counsel.

Phil sounds like he has concluded that it's best for Christians to avoid as much contact with the world as possible. He finds that the routine of daily life is inferior to maintaining a rigorous schedule of spiritual activities. The question this raises is: How much and to what level should I be interacting with the world? This is a complex topic, and one that has divided Christians throughout history.

During the Reformation of sixteenth-century Europe, a group sprang up called the Anabaptists. The name *Anabaptist* means "baptize again," given to them because they believed that infant baptism, the common practice in the Church, was insufficient. But many Anabaptists also believed that the Church should alienate itself from society as much as possible.

Back then, two Anabaptist men, both named Jan, tried to set up a Christian society in the German town of Munster. They thought if they could set up the perfect Christian establishment, free from the world's corruption, then that would be the place Christ would return to. They called this place "the New Jerusalem." But the society of their day wasn't prepared to accept this New Jerusalem, wanting their old Munster back instead. In a violent siege against the city of Munster, both Jans were killed.

Sometimes the Church becomes overly pious in relation to the world. Some people, like Phil and the two Jans, think that interaction with the world and its systems will only contaminate them.

Back in Colossae, there was also confusion over this issue of interaction with the world. Paul wrote to them and said,

Since, then, you have been raised with Christ, set your hearts on things above, where Christ is seated at the right hand of God. Set your minds on things above, not on earthly things (Colossians 3:1,2).

At first glance, this passage of Scripture seems to encourage action like Phil's and the Anabaptist men of Munster. Was the apostle Paul telling Christians to quit their jobs in order to spend all their time praying?

The answer to that question can be found in two phrases that he uses in this passage: "set your hearts" and "set your minds." The Colossians loved external shows of spirituality. But rather than shun reality by focusing on spiritual activities, they were to set the affections of their hearts on "the things above."

The Bible assumes that people will work to support themselves. In the Thessalonian church, some people had quit their jobs and were doing nothing but waiting for Christ's return. Paul told them that the one who doesn't work doesn't eat.

So although the Bible does teach us to avoid the world's sin, it does not teach us to avoid daily life. In fact, Jesus told His disciples that they were to be salt and light in the world. As salt is meant to season otherwise tasteless food, so Christ's disciples are called to affect the world we live in.

When Paul told the Colossians to set their minds on the things above, he called them to learn to love heaven more than their present life. They were to see that everything around them was temporary, and not worthy of their foremost love. Remember the basic Colossian problem of dethroning Christ? When the Christian exalts even spiritual activities above the Lord Jesus, the affections of his heart will be in the wrong place. So the Colossians needed to learn to love Jesus most, no matter what they were doing.

I will continue praying for you and Lee. I know that he is a hard worker, but I'm sure that once he learns to love Jesus most, his priorities will become different than they are now. As far as Phil is concerned, I can't judge him. But his solution to the problem of workaholism is only an external solution. I would sooner see the workaholic learn to love his work, but to love Jesus even more.

Your friend, Paul

Dear Paul,

I thought that Phil's solution for Lee sounded too other-worldly. Thanks for the confirmation. But after what happened this week, I'd bet that even Lee was tempted to quit his job.

Lee had a really bad experience with a Christian businessman. The guy owns a large business selling the same types of chemicals that Lee sells. His business has prospered, and he has become extremely rich. Lee came into contact with him when both were trying hard to sign a major customer. Lee had been working on this customer for a month, and was really close to signing him. But he found out later that the other guy had a spy checking on Lee's offer and terms. Once the rich businessman found out Lee's deal, he undercut him, stealing the customer.

This has seriously jeopardized Lee's chances of being named salesman of the year for his region. He was really upset about it, so he went to talk with the guy who undercut him. But Lee was even more upset after talking with him.

Lee couldn't believe it when the man said that he was a Christian. A Scripture hung just behind his desk, and Lee said it was something about letting justice roll down like the waters. Anyway, Lee just said that he didn't appreciate being cheated out of one of his biggest customers. Lee had spent a great deal of time trying to win this customer, and had lost out because the competition cheated.

Well, the businessman refused to admit any wrongdoing. He said that business is business. What he said next really infuriated Lee. The man said that he considered any increase of his business as a blessing from God. He told my husband that if he needed to argue with anyone, he needed to argue with God. Lee thought the guy was using this business triumph to prove that God was on his side.

He also found out that this guy is very active in politics. Another salesman later told Lee that this man spends a lot of time fund-raising and campaigning for Christian political candidates. Apparently he is quite well known in the Los Angeles area. Lee vowed that he would never vote for a candidate that this man supports. What do you think about these rich but unrighteous Christian businessmen and their political candidates?

I hope that this experience will not hinder my husband from becoming a Christian. I don't know if it will make him work harder to succeed or deflate him enough to slow him down for a while. It looks like his chances of getting salesman of the year are blown.

Your L.A. Onesimus

Dear Onesimus,

Christians have often had difficulties in places of power. In my last letter, I wrote to you about how the Christian should not avoid the world, but should be salt in his society. Unfortunately, society ends up affecting some Christians more than they season it.

The businessman you mentioned sounds like a crafty fellow. He has apparently stooped to using unrighteous techniques in business. Maybe he figures that it's the only way to get ahead and reach his aims. Perhaps he was even in Lee's place at one time, and learned that the only way to win the game was to play like the other big boys.

Power has often corrupted the Christian. The religious leaders of Spain in the fifteenth and sixteenth centuries called themselves Christians. They used their position as leaders to force Jews and Muslims either to be baptized or leave the country. Then, because the ones who chose baptism did not actually become zealous Christians, these religious leaders called for the Spanish Inquisition. During this time, the Christian leaders severely punished those suspected of being nominal Christians. These powerful leaders sought to convert the masses in a very ungodly way.

Christians often use the techniques of the world in the occupations they hold. Whether these people are businessmen or politicians, the temptation to love power and use it is great. Just look at how the sin of famous American television preachers has been hung before the American public like dirty laundry. For myself, I am not as disgusted by their actual sins of immorality as I am by their abuse of power.

The solution to this problem is the same as I mentioned in my last letter. The Christian must learn to set his affections on heaven. Christ said that we should lay up our treasures in heaven, because our hearts will be where our treasures are.

I believe it is wonderful if God exalts a Christian to the place of having political power. He did this a few times in the Bible with people like Joseph and Daniel. Then God used these ones to bless the nations they were serving, and especially to bless His own people in those nations. Both Daniel and Joseph maintained personal integrity, not allowing themselves to be corrupted by power.

But often, Christians in places of power have ended up discrediting their faith. This is what the businessman has done through his unrighteous actions toward Lee. Similarly, some television preachers have made the church look silly. They began to care more for their power than for the things of God.

But in the end, I wouldn't worry about this experience hindering Lee from becoming a Christian. After

all, he has a far better Christian witness living right under his own roof.

Your friend, Paul

Dear Paul,

The whole situation with the businessman actually ended up in my favor. I was sorry that Lee
had to go through that, but it has caused him to reflect
on things. He has begun to spend much more time at
home with his family.

We had Susan and her husband, Bob, over for dinner last night. This wasn't the first time Lee had met
Susan, but it was the first time for him to spend time
with Bob. As you know, Bob is a Christian, and I think
he may become Lee's first real friend in Los Angeles.
They both are interested in some of the same sports,
and they talked about them for hours. It was nice to see
Lee's mind off his work for a change.

After Bob and Susan left, Lee really opened up to
me about some of his struggles. He has tried so hard
this year, our first year in Los Angeles. When he didn't
land the big client he had spent so much time on, he really hit bottom emotionally. It made him think of my
previous talk with him, the time when I cried because
he was gone so much.

He has begun to ask himself about what's really important in life. He said that the emptiness he felt after
losing the client showed him that satisfaction from work
is a fleeting dream. He is also seeing that the future is always uncertain, and I think this scares him a little. It has

been many months since we had a talk like that.

I have appreciated your advice to me during this time. It has been important to learn about the Christian in relation to the world. I think it must be difficult to find the balance. I hope that Lee can become a Christian and learn that hard work does not have to control his life any more.

It seems like he's getting there. I continue to pray daily for him. I look forward to the first time we go to church together.

Your friend, Onesimus

Dear Onesimus,

ou mentioned the word balance, so I thought I should pen a few thoughts to you from Colossians. The Colossians had brought the techniques of other religions into the church. Because of this, they had lost sight of Jesus.

This is the chief danger for the Christian in relation to the world. More than affecting it, we more often are affected by the ideas and ways of the world. As I said in another letter, the solution to this problem lies in the heart of the Christian. He is to set his desires on heaven, his ultimate home. This was advice from Paul to the Colossians in the first four verses of chapter three.

I haven't made this clear to you yet, but Paul's exhortations here also deal with the ultimate end of the world. He said in verse four that "When Christ, who is your life, appears, you also will appear with him in glory." So when the believer sets his heart on the things of heaven, he is looking forward to the return of Christ.

Madeline, follow along in your Bible as I briefly tell you three things about Colossians 3:1-4. I believe that this passage helps us live a balanced Christian life in relation to the world. Each of these three points deal with the Christian's present life and circumstances.

First, the balanced Christian will understand his present position. The Colossians tried hard to get to the top, thinking that visions and rituals would plant them there. Today, many Christians also seek the glory of a high position. As you and Lee have learned, they often use the world's ways to get there.

We need to hear the reminder of Paul to the Colossians. Through Christ we are already at the top. We don't have to strive to achieve great status in anything. No matter what we accomplish in this life, we will never be higher than we already are. So because of his present position, the Christian shouldn't strive to be promoted.

Second, the balanced Christian understands his present action. He is seeking Christ more than he is seeking a secondary experience or specific function. Paul wanted the Colossians to do one thing in relation to their spirituality: set their minds on Christ. This is the basic command in Colossians.

This command teaches that we need to use our new eyes. In another letter, Paul prayed for the Church that God would enlighten the eyes of their hearts (Ephesians 1:18). When God does that, the Christian more clearly sees the things he should be seeing.

When the Communists invaded Afghanistan and ordered the closure of all churches, one church did something which showed their hearts' eyes had been opened. As workers were destroying the church with bulldozers, church members took trays of cookies to them. The workers began to cry, ashamed that they had to destroy the property of such good people. Those church members were, through this action, witnessing to the bulldozer operators. Their affections were set on the things of Christ more than on a physical church building.

Third, the balanced Christian understands his present hope. The Bible teaches that the hope of the future will affect our present situation. The book of Hebrews says that Abraham lived in tents rather than a regular house, because he looked forward to a better future. The hope of heaven affected him by causing him to be less concerned about his physical comfort.

So, Madeline, I pray that this hope would be placed firmly in your heart and in Lee's. Even if all his business ventures fail (but I pray that they will succeed), you can always do what Abraham did. There are probably lots of places to pitch a tent around Los Angeles.

Your friend, Paul

8

How Spiritual People Deal With Sin

Dear Paul,

I have no more progress reports on Lee, though I'm certainly glad he didn't come with me to church yesterday. I'm not sure he would have come back again.

We had only a short time of singing this week before the main pastor announced that the youth pastor had something to share. Since I began attending the Christian Fellowship, I usually have enjoyed listening to the youth pastor speak. He's interesting and dynamic. This week his wife was sitting up on the platform as well, which wasn't the norm. At first, though, I didn't think too much about it.

When the youth pastor came to the front and I could see his face, I knew something was wrong. His red, puffy eyes showed that he had been crying. He stood in front of the pulpit for what seemed like five minutes before saying anything. A longer look at his wife revealed the same red, swollen eyes. I realized that something was wrong, and the silence began to feel awkward.

Finally the youth pastor began to speak. He confessed to a series of adulterous relationships, not naming any of the women involved. In a broken voice, he asked for the church's forgiveness and said how much he had appreciated his wife during this time. I thought to myself that he chose a fine way to express his appreciation. Anyway, when he referred to his wife, she raised her head from its bowed position and flashed him a smile. Then he broke down in tears, and the rest of the church staff surrounded him for prayer.

The pastor spoke that morning on accepting the repentant sinner no matter what they had done. I guess I can see the truth of that. But the fact that this guy committed adultery with several different women, and had totally covered it up, really repulsed me. And to think that he had been one of the church leaders, as well!

Some of the parents, especially those with kids in the youth group, are angry with the situation. It sounds like some are going to leave the church, hoping to find a place with a better influence for their kids. I've heard that they don't feel that the youth pastor has received sufficient retribution for his sin.

I'm not sure how to feel about the whole thing. I can see the pastor's point about accepting and forgiving the sinner. But how can anyone be sure that the guy isn't just going to do it all over again? And how does this jive with the Gospel? I mean, Lee isn't a Christian, and I know that he's far from perfect, but I also know that he's not an adulterer. I would far sooner have him for a husband, Christian or not, than someone I may not be able to depend on.

So what is the right response in this situation? I think of Sunset, the girl I spoke with right after moving to Los Angeles. At the time I confronted her on her immoral lifestyle. Little would I know that a year later, one of my church leaders would have the same problem.

Your L.A. Onesimus

Dear Onesimus,

I can understand your feeling of shock after being let down by a church leader you had respected. I have experienced this same feeling many times. The Dean of my Bible school (a very conservative and Christ-centered school) even left his wife for a younger woman. Prior to his adultery, he was a popular, international Bible teacher and a wonderful school leader. His sin surprised us students, I suppose partly because we felt that he somehow represented God to us. It was difficult to imagine him having this weakness.

Once you get over the shock of hearing this sad news about the youth pastor, I want to encourage you to respond with love to him. After all, the youth pastor, the head pastor, or any church leader is no more immune to sin than anyone else. At this point, the youth pastor recognizes his sin, and it sounds like he really wants to change. The church needs to surround him with open hands, offering acceptance, rather than with clenched fists that seek to punish.

Madeline, you asked in your letter how this man's sin jives with the Gospel. Let me explain some things about sin to you. So far in Los Angeles, you have met a couple of people with different views on sin. To the New Age girl, Sunset, sin is anything that her own conscience doesn't like. Therefore, she can live as immorally as her conscience permits. To the perfectionist, June Graham, sin is comparable to law-keeping. She thought she had kept the Law without error for four months.

The Colossian church also viewed sin as the breaking of external rules. These rules, imposed on them by culture or religion, included things like Jewish cleanliness and dietary laws. They thought that eating or touching certain things would be sin. But Paul told them that external rules cannot restrain sensual indulgences (Colossians 2:20-23), the heart of sin. Having the appearance of moral perfection may appear spiritual, but true spirituality is found far below the surface.

Your church's youth pastor possibly has a sexual addiction. It is obvious that he earnestly desires fellowship with his wife and the church. He has probably been very frustrated with his inability to do the right thing, to keep the biblical rules of sexual conduct. Perhaps those who listened closely to his heart on the Sunday he shared perceived this frustration.

Paul said to the Colossians, "Put to death, therefore, whatever belongs to your earthly nature: sexual immorality, impurity, lust, evil desires and greed, which is idolatry" (Colossians 3:5). The words *put to death* could also be translated *kill*. The Bible assumes that every human being, Christians included, own a sinful nature. We are commanded to wage war against it, constantly seeking to kill our sinful nature like a warrior attempting to vanquish his enemy.

Madeline, I want you to notice the first words Paul used in this passage to describe the sinful nature: *sexual immorality, impurity,* and *passion.* The fact that sexual sins are common to the sinful nature of mankind is testified to by countless stories of sin and failure.

I recently read about a convention held for Christians. When checking which movies they had watched while staying in the convention hotel, it was discovered that many of them had watched a pornographic movie. These were Christian men and women, actively engaged in ministry, committing sexual sin.

If I had time, and if it were edifying, I could give you many such statistics and tell many stories describing the moral failures of church leadership. As I said, sexual impurity is one aspect of sinful human nature, common to all mankind since Adam's fall. Even one of the most respected and humble men of God in the entire Bible, King David, committed a very serious sexual sin. He even covered it up, like the youth pastor did, for a long time.

You may remember that in another letter, I told you about Origen, the famous third-century theologian. He tried to rid himself of all sexual inclinations by castrating himself. This is not the Bible's way of dealing with the sin nature. We are told to go below the physical surface to the very roots of our sinful nature. At these roots, we feel the *desire* to sin, and this is what we are to kill. The sin nature usually does not die quickly or easily. The battle may take much time and energy. And it is won by looking back to the work Christ did for us on the Cross, the time when He declared victory over all of our sin.

I think your youth pastor has taken an important practical step by admitting his sin to the church. In essence, he knows that he has a problem and that he needs help. I think that his confession of shame before the church is an indication that he has already done that before God. I hope that most of the church members will help him in his fight against his sin nature. This is a crucial time for him. His willpower is insufficient to fight the sin of sexual indulgence. He will need much grace and power from God, and much love and support from his church family.

About Lee, if he had come to church with you that day, perhaps he would have responded in a way that would have surprised you. Remember, he was repulsed by the hypocrisy of the Christian businessman. Maybe he needs to see an honest Christian who has failed and is crying out for help.

Your friend, Paul

Dear Paul,

*I*t's interesting that you should mention the Christian businessman again. Just yesterday, Lee brought it up in conversation again. He says that every time he thinks of the crooked businessman, he gets an upset stomach.

He went on to talk about the businessman in relation to Christianity. He doesn't understand how someone could call himself a Christian, yet be more shady in business than people who don't call themselves Christians. I didn't think that this talk was an appropriate time to tell him about the youth pastor.

I continue to hope that Lee's experience with the businessman will not deter him from becoming a Christian himself. But I don't understand it very well, either. I do understand what you said in your last letter about dealing with the heart of sin. I can see that the youth pastor knows he has a deep problem that he is fighting against. But this businessman didn't even seem to realize that his business dealings were sinful. He even thought that his success gained through unethical practices proved God's blessing on his life.

How can someone like this call himself a Christian? Doesn't his presence in church make a mockery of the entire institution?

By the way, Lee did get his minor bonus, but didn't make salesman of the year. In the end, though, I don't think he really cared that much.

Your L.A. Onesimus

Dear Onesimus,

There is an important difference between the businessman and the youth pastor. One cares about his sin while the other does not. Being concerned or sorrowful about one's sin is an important part of killing it.

In my last letter I directed you to Colossians 3:5 where Paul told the Colossians, "Put to death, therefore, whatever belongs to your earthly nature: sexual immorality, impurity, lust, evil desires and greed, which is idolatry." We looked at the first three sins, the ones of the sexual nature. The next aspects of the earthly nature deal with the other sin you have witnessed in a Christian, namely, greed.

Do not come to the conclusion that this businessman is not a Christian simply because he has not overcome this sin. From the way you have described him, he is unaware of this part of his sinful nature. God must open the man's eyes to see into his own heart of sin.

Remember that I said the Colossians tried to be spiritual and pure by following rules. In other words, they relied on their willpower to fight against their concept of sin. But Paul told them that in doing this, they were not going to the heart of the problem.

The businessman, once he is aware of his sin, will need to treat it like the youth pastor is treating his sexual sin: as a part of his sinful character, deeply embedded in his heart. His crooked business dealings are motivated by greed, and this is found deep down in his heart. Like the youth pastor, this businessman must be changed by the power of the Cross.

Jesus worked with twelve disciples who each had various character problems. Because of fear, each of them deserted Jesus when He needed them most. They had spent a few years following the Lord, hearing His teaching, and watching His miracles. But they didn't really change until after Jesus had died and was resurrected. The sin of greed was deeply ingrained in the character of one disciple, Judas. Unfortunately, he wasn't around after Christ's death and resurrection to receive the power necessary to change his wicked heart.

I believe that greed is as serious a problem in the Church as sexual immorality. It is even displayed by church leaders who have become rich and powerful. I once heard of an itinerant evangelist who traveled to his crusades in one of his two private jets. He said he bought those planes because he found it difficult to pray and listen to God on the commercial flights with people smoking around him. Greed is also evident in others, like businessmen who make unethical business deals. And it is seen in the hearts of all Christians who close their hearts to the poor.

In time, you will stop feeling surprised when you see Christians fail, especially in the areas of sexual immorality and greed. These two basic parts of fallen humanity are found deep inside, and only a humbling confrontation with the Cross will rid us of these sins.

Though man is sinful, that is not an excuse we can offer God for committing sin. Christ died on the cross to deal a death blow to our sin. This is why Paul commanded the Colossians to put these sinful tendencies to death. If not, they were promised that God's wrath would visit them (Colossians 3:6).

When Lee does make a commitment to Christ, he will be able to see the businessman with new eyes. He will see the sinfulness of his own character, and will be more able to identify with the one who cheated him. The sincere Christian understands the depravity of his own heart, and therefore can sympathize with others in their shortcomings.

Your friend, Paul

Dear Paul,

*T*hanks for helping me find some perspective on the nature of sin. I wish you had been at our

Care Group this week. You would have seen that I wasn't the only one surprised by the youth pastor's adulterous relationships.

The most vocal of the group was, as usual, Larry. He wanted to discuss the youth pastor's problem and offer a solution as to why it happened in the first place. He reckons that the youth pastor wasn't reading his Bible enough. If he had been, reasoned Larry, then God's Word would automatically have made him strong. Larry says that his own life motto is, "A chapter a day keeps the devil away."

Different ones in the group also wanted to talk about the situation. In fact, I have never seen our Care Group participate so enthusiastically in any discussion as I did that night. There were a few, as well, who are still very angry about the entire situation. They think that the youth pastor should receive the boot, or that at least he should move far away to have this problem dealt with.

Phil, the guy who quit his job and lives off the government, feels that the youth pastor had given too much of himself to his work and not enough of himself to God. This input was to be expected from Phil. But the one who really surprised me was Jim, the Care Group leader. He said that he had not trusted the youth group pastor ever since the church first hired him. He went on to say that he feels like the man is superficial, lacking any spiritual depth. This was quite a mouthful coming from Jim, our normally quiet and very tolerant leader.

By the time the meeting was over, the youth pastor had been pretty much raked over the coals. I felt sorry for him, even though he wasn't there and was unaware of the things said.

If you had been at the meeting, you probably would have rebuked everyone for kicking a man when he's down. What do you think about all this talk? I guess that this week, "Care Group" may not be the most appropriate name for our fellowship.

Your L.A. Onesimus

Dear L.A. Onesimus,

*T*his month you have certainly seen the underside of the church. Your experience in the Care Group allowed you to witness in Christians another aspect of the sinful heart. This aspect is found in wrong attitudes and speech.

I suppose if I had been with the group, I may have, as you suggested, rebuked everyone for kicking a man when he's down. But I would have gone further than that. I would have drawn them, like I have done for you over the past year, to the book of Colossians. The apostle Paul told the church to rid themselves of anger, rage, malice, slander, and filthy language (Colossians 3:8). Like Larry with his "chapter a day" rule, the Colossian church had provided simplistic and superficial solutions for sin. But when they slandered each other, it became clear that they hadn't really dealt with the heart of sin.

Christians often like to assign types of sin to various levels of sinfulness. The youth pastor has committed, in the minds of many Christians, one of the worst sins imaginable—adultery. To these same Christians, the deceitful businessman is probably not quite as bad, though his sin does deserve some dishonorable mention. And mention it they will, not once bothering to think that their discussion itself equals sin. Slander is a sin that grieves God, especially when it is committed against a brother in Christ.

Your Care Group must learn to take this sin very seriously, and each of the members must seek to kill it in their hearts. They need to see that their penchant for slander only reveals that they are a part of sinful mankind, sons of Adam and brothers to the adulterous youth pastor and the deceitful businessman. If they can see themselves clearly through this situation, they will have an opportunity to do what the youth pastor has already embarked on. They, too, will want to wage war on their sinful nature.

Remember, Colossians teaches that our sin is nailed to the cross with Christ. We were once dead in sin but God made us alive together with Christ. Our sin once made us dead people, but Christ took this sinful body of death and crucified it (Colossians 2:13,14; 3:3). Our responsibility is to absolutely mortify it, not allowing it to live and control us.

Madeline, do you remember that you once were going to make an unexpected preaching debut at the Care Group? At that time, you didn't have to because the Lord Himself preached the message He wanted the group to hear. Well, maybe this is another chance for you. Try to show them how awful the sin of slander is. And if you are guilty of any yourself, then you can begin your sermon with a confession.

Your good friend, Paul

9

How Spiritual People
Treat Others

Dear Paul,

Thanks for helping me find the right perspective on sin. And thanks for the advice in your past three letters, though I don't plan to latch on to the bit about preaching too soon. I realize now that our Care Group has some problems, but I would prefer to have Jesus preach the message to them again. They have become like a family to me here (like you all were in Boston), and I would hate to ruin that.

Now I need some more advice. Susan has made a plan for her and me to go to the youth pastor's house for lunch. She spent some time chatting with his wife after church on Sunday. Susan says that she left the conversation feeling like the person who is blameless in this situation has somehow been the one to receive the most pain. Anyway, during their conversation, Susan tried to encourage her, and the wife asked her to come for lunch one day. Susan asked her if I could come, too. Susan thinks it would be a good idea if we could show both the youth pastor and his wife that we care.

Well, I have two problems with this. First, let me make it clear that I do care about the woman's situation. It makes me sick when I think about the grief she must be going through. But I honestly would not have a clue about what I should say to them. I mean, this lady and her husband were in a position of church leadership before I was even a Christian. What good could I be to them? And what if I said something dumb that only made the situation worse? I guess deep down, I honestly still wonder why she didn't just dump the guy. Sitting at the same lunch table with him would, I think, be a very uncomfortable experience.

My second problem is, I realize, more superficial. I am wondering how the Care Group would respond if Susan and I spent time with these people. The group is already divided over how the church should have dealt with the youth pastor. I would hate to bring more division into my fellowship family. I guess I also care quite deeply about being accepted by the Care Group.

Is there anything that absolutely requires me to go for lunch with the youth pastor and his wife? In some ways I would like to, but I guess I just see that the problems outweigh any possible good I could do. Maybe Susan, a more mature Christian, should just go alone and it could be kept quiet from the Care Group.

I realize that this is not the most earth-shattering decision that's ever been made, but I have lost one night's sleep over it. I feel that if I don't go, I will appear callous, but if I do go, I may do more harm than good.

When I first heard the youth pastor admit his sin, I had no idea that it would affect me, too. This whole situation is becoming too uncomfortable.

Your L.A. Onesimus

Dear Onesimus,

*F*irst, let me put your heart at ease by saying that etiquette does not require you to have lunch with the youth pastor and his wife, if that's what you are asking. If you didn't have lunch with them, it wouldn't be considered a social blunder. Now that you are breathing a sigh of relief over that one, let me also say that you have been given the mind of Christ. Often the mind of Christ will teach us to do things contrary to what our own hearts tell us.

After Paul wrote the Colossian church about the heart of sin (the things they *shouldn't* be doing), he explained right Christian conduct (the things they *should* be doing). These were active stances that they could take for the welfare of other people.

Therefore, as God's chosen people, holy and dearly loved, clothe yourselves with compassion, kindness, humility, gentleness and patience. Bear with each other and forgive whatever grievances you may have against one another. Forgive as the Lord forgave you. And over all these virtues put on love, which binds them all together in perfect unity (Colossians 3:12-14).

Notice that Paul encouraged the Colossians to clothe themselves. We wear clothing for the sake of other people. If there were only one human being on planet Earth, chances are that he wouldn't wear clothes. In the same way, virtues like compassion, kindness, humility, gentleness, patience, and forgiveness are useless without someone to show them to.

This Scripture should help you make your decision about whether or not to visit the youth pastor and his wife. I won't tell you what to do in this situation. Instead, I think that by thoughtfully reflecting on this Scripture, you will be able to make the right decision. The very first items of spiritual clothing for Christians are compassion and kindness. These are two things that I can guarantee the youth pastor and his wife need at this time.

The text here also speaks of forgiveness. The youth pastor's wife doesn't need the church's forgiveness, because she hasn't offended the church. But her husband does. Perhaps in reaching out to both of them, people at the Christian Fellowship can also send the message of forgiveness to the husband.

One of the most powerful stories about forgiveness I have ever heard happened a few decades ago. In the 1950s, a group of five missionary men went to share Christ with a previously unreached native tribe, the Aucas of South America. Not only had this tribe never been reached with the Gospel, it also had very little contact with the outside world. But after the five men landed their small plane, the natives met them with fierce hostility. Before the missionaries could share anything about Christ, the tribe killed each one. One of the men, Jim Elliot, had only been married a short time.

A few years later, Jim's young widow, Elisabeth, felt that God wanted her to go back to this tribe and finish the job her husband had started. The way was paved for her by an Auca woman named Dayuma. Elisabeth was accompanied by Rachel Saint, the sister of one of the other dead missionaries. Slowly the Auca Indians of South America, a tribe that had previously murdered many more outsiders than these five missionaries, became receptive to Christ. A church was begun among them, and the tribe was evangelized.

Elisabeth Elliot and Rachel Saint chose to dress themselves in forgiveness for the sake of the people who had killed their loved ones. Partly because of their decision to put on the right spiritual clothing, an extremely hostile tribe came to know Christ. In the same way, if your church family can practice forgiveness toward the youth pastor, it will result in the kind of reconciliation that Christ died for.

You will notice that I have nowhere said what you should do in this lunch situation. But I do have full confidence that you will do the right thing.

Your friend, Paul

Dear Paul,

*B*efore your last letter, I had never been told so clearly what to do without being told what to do. I took your advice, the advice you said you didn't give, and accompanied Susan to the youth pastor's house for lunch. It turned out that half of my fears were in vain, because the youth pastor was out meeting with one of the other church pastors. But Susan and I enjoyed a very meaningful lunch with his wife.

Perhaps, as you said, she did need the compassion

and kindness of two people showing her that they care. But I think she encouraged us far more than we encouraged her. She admitted that she feels very hurt over the whole situation, feeling like her husband chose other women over her. But at the same time, she says that she didn't have any problem at all forgiving him. In fact, she felt more compassion for him than she felt hurt for herself. I can now understand why her husband said that day how much he appreciated his wife.

Her deep and unselfish love amazed, encouraged, and motivated me. After lunch Susan and I agreed that the slanderous talk our Care Group had indulged in was totally uncalled for. I decided to take your advice and preach to the group. I began by apologizing to them for slandering the youth pastor and his wife, both in my heart and with my lips. I then read that passage from Colossians, and shared a little about why I feel slander is wrong. I also told the group about our lunch with the wife, and shared some of her needs with them.

My defensive side expected the Care Group to respond with an argument. But they seemed genuinely moved by my words. A few even joined me in admitting that they were wrong by slandering the youth pastor. But to be honest, I didn't really care that much about how the group responded. I just knew that I was doing the right thing.

Apart from you, I can't think of another Christian who has moved me as much as the wife we had lunch with. If Lee could see that kind of unselfish love in me, I know he would become a Christian. But if he ever does anything to give me that kind of opportunity to love him unselfishly, I think I would kill him.

Your L.A. Onesimus

Dear Onesimus,

*I*t's great that you took the bold step to set yourself apart from the sin of your Care Group! I believe that you will see the fruit of your actions in the weeks to come.

It is always encouraging to see someone who loves much. You said that the wife's love amazed, encouraged, and motivated you. Just think how much more the twelve disciples of Christ would have been motivated by the perfect love they saw continually in their Lord.

When Paul discussed spiritual clothing with the Colossians, he said to put love on over everything else. He said that love binds everything together. Love is the thing that keeps us in balance. If perfect love motivates us, we can be sure of our actions. With love we can rebuke and forgive someone at the same time without being schizophrenic. At no time did you say that you felt the wife's love was born out of naivete or tolerance. Certainly the love that forgives her husband also demands moral purity from him.

Perhaps by your sharing with your Care Group, this type of pure, unselfish love will be held up as an ideal. This love, said Paul, is the thing that binds everything together in perfect unity. In another letter, he encouraged the Church to walk in love as Christ did, by sacrificing himself for other people.

True, unselfish love always motivates people. After the five young men were killed by the Auca Indians of South America, many Christians decided to give their lives to missions. Those Christians who have suffered because of their deep love for other people always motivate the rest of the Church.

I trust that Lee will not provide you the opportunity to love him unselfishly like the youth pastor did for his wife. Still, you needn't wait for a personal crisis before displaying unselfish love. If you are in the habit of loving sacrificially every day, it will be second nature to you when the really difficult times require it of you.

Your friend, Paul

10

How Spiritual People Reach Out

Dear Paul,

I was happy to get your letter this week. The comments you made about love touched me. Yesterday, I also received another piece of mail from some people who say they want to help my prayer life. I have no idea how they got my name.

Their help came in the form of something they call the "Bible Prayer Rug." The rug is a doormat-sized piece of fabric with a picture of Jesus stitched on it. They sent me a rug which they claim has the power to bless, and a long letter on how to use it. They said that I could pray for whatever I want, be it joy, peace, health, a new car, or a new house. If I pray while kneeling on the prayer rug, or if the prayer rug covers my knees when I pray, I will receive what I am praying for.

They made it clear that I should send the rug back to them the next day. They were quite insistent about this, mentioning it at least three times in the letter, as if the rug would start bringing bad luck on the second day. They also said that I should lay my wallet on the prayer rug, pray for financial multiplication, and then take out my largest bill to send to them. A testimony from a certain Sister Garcia was enclosed. She said that she had tried this method, sent the owners $50, and God gave her more than $46,000 back.

I am not writing to you to ask for advice on whether or not to use this prayer rug. I have learned enough by being with Christians for the past year to be able to spot a Colossian. And I have seen enough just as a human being to know a scam when I see one. Actually, I am offended that someone gave these people my name. Whoever that was must have thought I would be gullible enough to swallow it. I returned the prayer rug to the sender the same day I got it. I didn't even add postage. I just sealed it back up and wrote "Return to Sender" on the envelope.

The situation, though, did cause me to reflect on my own prayer life. As it seems that so often my prayers remain unanswered, I have begun wondering if I am doing something wrong. I have prayed that Andrew would be healed from his asthma nearly every day since his first trip to the hospital here. But he hasn't improved one iota. Doesn't the Bible say that if somebody is righteous, and they pray constantly, their prayers will have a great effect? Why do my prayers seem so completely ineffective?

I am also continuing to pray that Lee would get saved, but he seems in about the same place spiritually as before. Sometimes I get discouraged by the lack of progress I see. Nearly every week in Care Group, Larry, the visionary, gives some testimony about how God has answered his prayers. To be honest, his answers to prayer sometimes seem like the natural outworking of circumstances. But I wonder if in his quacky system of spirituality he doesn't somehow have a better handle on effective praying.

Your L.A. Onesimus

Dear Onesimus,

*T*he Church today has various strange concepts about prayer. I think the prayer rug scheme may win in a contest of bizarre ideas on prayer. A close second may be an idea I heard about a few years ago. These people felt that they should charter a plane to fly over the Soviet Union, with the goal of praying for the release of Soviet Jews. They believed that, since the battle is fought in the heavenlies, being 30,000 feet up in an airplane would make their prayers especially effective.

I am happy to help you in this crucial area of life. The Bible teaches about prayer in several places. In your last letter to me, you mentioned the passage from James chapter five that says that the prayer of a righteous man is powerful and effective. When Paul explained church order to the struggling pastor Timothy, he said that the foremost thing to consider is prayer (I Timothy 2:1).

You can find much teaching on prayer in the Bible, and you can find many characters who had strong prayer lives. In fact, Samuel (of the Old Testament) even considered it sin to not pray for his people. But I won't take you on a study through those teachings and characters. Since you have been my Onesimus over the past year, let's look together again in the book of Colossians. There the apostle Paul also gave a basic lesson on prayer.

Devote yourselves to prayer, being watchful and thankful. And pray for us, too, that God may open a door for our message, so that we may proclaim the mystery of Christ, for which I am in chains (Colossians 4:2,3).

Notice two things that Paul taught the Colossians about prayer. First, he said that Christians should devote themselves to prayer. What are we doing when we devote ourselves to prayer? We are bringing ourselves near to God, stating to him that we rely on Him. Whether we are greatly needy or just thankful, we pray because we lack the resources to handle life without God. You are continuing to pray for both Lee and Andrew because you know that ultimately, God is the One who can help them both. The Christian who forgets to pray believes subconsciously that his activity is more important than God's.

During the last century, the heart of Englishman George Muller became broken for the orphans of his country. Muller decided to open orphanages for them, even though he didn't have any assets with which to help the children. But he decided to throw in his lot with the orphans and learn to rely on God for both his needs and theirs. For forty years, George Muller supplied homes, food, and a living for orphans. Muller constantly testified that his homes were maintained only by prayer. He prayed daily that God would supply the needs for the orphans and the homes.

This is what it means to devote oneself to prayer. Of course, you don't need to start orphanages before you can devote yourself to prayer. You can learn this lesson right now in your present circumstances. And you are learning it. I urge you never to grow weary of praying for those close to you. Give yourself to pray for them.

Second, Paul encouraged the Colossians to be thankful in prayer. This is a very easy concept to apply. Madeline, you can think of many things in life to be thankful for, including your husband, children, home, church, and so on. Take time daily to think about the things you are grateful for, the people in your life, and the things that God allows you to experience. Tell God, the giver of all good gifts, the things that you appreciate.

The Bible teaches that we are to give thanks for all things. This means that we are to thank God for the most difficult people and things in life. It took me a few months, but I finally told God "Thank You" for taking Gracie from me and bringing her home to be with Him. You will want to thank him for Larry, the home group visionary, and even for that Christian businessman who cheated Lee. Perhaps God is using that situation to bring Lee into His family.

Madeline, it is crucial that you learn the practice of prayer, the life of dependence on God. You don't need anything to be an effective praying person other than more practice. Don't be intimidated by all of Larry's answers to prayer. I find that Colossians are often quick to testify to answered prayers, genuine or not, because it makes them appear more spiritual, like they have a clearer connection to God than others.

A successful prayer life takes practice. You don't need to be in a closet with a prayer rug or circling the world in an airplane. To pray, you just need to be with

God, and that, my dear, is wherever you are.

Your friend, Paul

Dear Paul,

This week I received the most exciting answer to prayer that I could have hoped for. I am now part of a bona fide Christian couple. Yes, it's true. Lee made a commitment to Christ two days ago.

Bob and Susan came over for dinner again that night. After the children went out to play, the four of us sat in the living room with our coffee. Bob began talking about his brother, and how empty his life is even though he's made it to the top of his field. Although he is so much richer than Bob and Susan, he envies their contentment.

Lee really surprised me by opening up to the three of us. He said that he can relate to Bob's brother. He had been trying so hard in his work until that businessman cheated him. Lee said that, though he still reflects on the situation quite often, he doesn't really think about the businessman any more. Now he just thinks about how empty the whole work-eat-sleep cycle is.

Bob went on to share that Lee is empty because God has created him for something more than being a chemical salesman. He explained that God wants a relationship with people, and that everyone shares the same void until God fills it. Even though I have been praying for Lee for more than a year, I was totally surprised when he invited Christ into his life. He confessed his sin before us all, and told God that he needed Him. Lee even cried, something I have never seen him do before.

It goes without saying that I am the happiest I have been since moving to Los Angeles. Tomorrow is Sunday, the first day that we will go to church as a family.

Lee is very happy, and is more content than I have ever seen him. He and Bob have made a plan to meet once each week for Bible study and prayer. He already wants to share Christ with other people. I heard him telling Charlie, our agnostic neighbor, about how happy he is that he has made a decision to become a Christian. Lee isn't the least bit shy about it. Maybe together we can really start reaching people here in La-La Land for Christ.

About the prayer rug, I discovered that other people in the Care Group had been sent the same rug. It turned out that Larry receives regular literature from the owners of the rug, and he sent them the names and addresses of the entire Care Group. It all made sense to me after that. I could see the relationship between these people and Larry, even without one of your letters pointing it out to me.

Your L.A. Onesimus

Dear Onesimus,

I share your deep joy over Lee's salvation. You now have received a great answer to prayer that will motivate you to keep praying for people. Even though Lee is your husband, you have had to act toward him like someone outside the Church family. The Bible teaches Christians how to relate to those outside the

Church, often with the hope of winning them to Christ.

Paul also shared some brief teaching with the Colossians on how to act toward those outside the Church. He said, "Be wise in the way you act toward outsiders; make the most of every opportunity. Let your conversation be always full of grace, seasoned with salt, so that you may know how to answer everyone." Here he encouraged the church in a lifestyle of evangelism, showing forth Christ through their Christian character.

Although Bob shared some brief words of the salvation message, you have been the primary evangelist in Lee's life. I can guarantee that it has been your wise actions, gracious speech, and constant prayers that God used to speak to Lee's heart. So you need no lesson on evangelism. Keep being like Christ before others, and like Lee, they will be attracted to the beauty of Jesus.

Make the most of every opportunity to show the life of Christ in your actions. That reminds me of a story I heard a few years ago. The evangelist and teacher Larry Tomczak had been holding meetings in a certain city. Later, he got on a bus to go home. He paid the bus driver for the fare, and the driver handed him some change. Walking back to his seat, Larry counted the change and discovered that the driver had given him too much. He went back and handed the excess change to the driver. The driver said that he gave Larry too much change on purpose. You see, he, too, had attended one of Larry's meetings, and wanted to see if the evangelist truly practiced the things he was preaching.

The world is watching us. It is our job to show them what our Lord is like. You have done a good job so far. Keep it up.

Your friend, Paul

Dear Paul,

This has been quite an interesting sixteen months in La-La Land. When we moved here, I was so depressed that I didn't know if I would live through the first two weeks without having a nervous breakdown.

For a long time, it didn't seem that I would ever find a church fellowship like the one I shared with you and the others in Boston. The first Christians I met in Los Angeles told me that I was possessed by demons. That was not exactly the comfort I was looking for during my initial days in this new city.

I can look back now and see that even though these sixteen months have had their painful moments, I have grown immensely during them. I have met some unique people, inside and outside the Church. These people, even with their bizarre views of spirituality, have caused me to reflect on my own spiritual life.

Of course the greatest blessing is that my family now has a Christian husband and father. Lee is growing quickly, and his enthusiasm challenges me. As a couple, we have so much more to talk about now. Before I couldn't really share with him about my experiences with Christians in Los Angeles. First, he wouldn't have had anything to say about it, other than probably a dis-gusted grunt. Second, I didn't want to turn him off from Christ by telling about the weird Christians I was meeting.

Your letters have been a mainstay for me. I have en-joyed being your Onesimus out here in La-La Land. You were right—this is a spiritual Disneyland. But thanks to your constant reminders about the Headship of Christ, I have begun to realize which rides I should avoid.

Your L.A. Onesimus

Dear Onesimus,

*I*t has been thrilling for me to watch you from a distance, surviving all your bumpy rides in Disneyland. You have done well; your faith in Christ has remained strong.

Continue to be aware of the Colossians around you. Remember, they are the ones who emphasize spiritual methods, techniques, and programs while de-emphasizing the message of Christ and the Cross. You have met some already, and they have made you question your own spirituality. Always remember that you are spiritual through Christ, as He is the fullness of everything.

Doubtless there are many more Colossians waiting in the wings in your future. They seem to be everywhere in the Church these days. But one of the greatest dangers of Colossian influence is found within ourselves. We often hear about other Christians who have had visionary experiences or healing, and then we doubt our own level of spirituality. At times we may seek to make up for what we deem a spiritual deficit in ourselves through activities that we think are spiritual. Your prayer life, visions you receive, doing evangelism, praying for the sick—none of these things will make you spiritual. Jesus has made you spiritual, and therefore you will want to pray for the lost, pray for the sick, do evangelism, cast out demons, and possibly receive visions.

So, my Onesimus, the church will throw a lot of ideas at you, some of them incorrect ones. Keep looking to Jesus as the Author and Perfecter of your faith. In His light, the pressures of Colossae will melt into a puddle of trivial exercises.

So as Paul said to the Colossians , I say to you:

As you received Christ Jesus as Lord, continue to live in him, rooted and built up in him, strengthened in the faith as you were taught, and overflowing with thankfulness (Colossians 2:6).

Your friend, Paul